HUMAN GENETICS
A Christian Perspective

edited by

William Storrar and Iain Torrance

Credits

General Editors: Hugh Brown and Kristine Gibbs.
Design concept: Mark Blackadder.
Photographs: *Daily Telegraph* Colour Library (front cover) and Camilla Jessel (back cover).
Typeset in Palatino and Helvetica.

Published on behalf of:
The CHURCH of SCOTLAND
BOARD of SOCIAL RESPONSIBILITY
47 Milton Road East, Edinburgh EH15 2SR
by SAINT ANDREW PRESS
121 George Street, Edinburgh EH2 4YN.

Copyright © 1995
The CHURCH of SCOTLAND
BOARD of SOCIAL RESPONSIBILITY.

British Library Cataloguing in Publication Data
A catalogue record for this book is available from the British Library.

ISBN 0861532082

Printed and **bound** in Scotland by Fingerprint (Scotland) Ltd, Livingston.

Foreword

This is a book which will appeal to anyone who seeks to be informed about a complex subject. Human genetics receives continuous attention in the press and media. It influences the life of many people directly, and as a result of professional practice which may develop without public comment unless society takes the trouble to be informed.

The book first of all sets the scene and highlights that while it is possible to envisage a future in which the excesses of genetic manipulation are possible, the likelihood is that developments which are market-driven are more probable. The scientific perspective enables the lay reader to understand enough about the subject to then put the debate into perspective; this is an invaluable section which stimulates as well as informs. In a similar manner the pastoral perspective enables the reader to place the human issues against the scientific facts and within a Christian perspective.

For many readers the most demanding section of the book will be the theological perspective. Their understanding will be influenced by their present knowledge base. Those who have a background or knowledge of theology will find this chapter an excellent exposition of a particular perspective. The book would be incomplete without it. The section on public and ethical perspectives highlights many of the issues that will be with us into the new millennium.

I am delighted with this production and I am sure that it will become a key publication on Human Genetics. The General Assembly of the Church of Scotland in May 1995 welcomed the Report on which this book is based.

Ian D Baillie
Director of Social Work

Preface

Human genetics affects us all. It is changing the way we all look at human life, and understand ourselves. Quite rightly, many people are looking to the Church for guidance and support.

This 1995 Church of Scotland Report has been produced by the Board of Social Responsibility and its Study Group on Human Genetics. It offers an informed, balanced account of current scientific and medical developments and a realistic view of what may be possible or likely within human genetics in the foreseeable future, taking account of how research is funded and managed. It can only be a snapshot in time in what is a rapidly changing field of research. But the Report sees this changing scene from an enduring Christian perspective that we believe can cope with the new and unexpected.

After an introductory scientific account of human genetics in chapter 2, recent public discussion of the ethical issues is set within that distinctive Christian perspective in chapter 3. This leads on to the Report's guiding vision in chapter 4, where life is seen as both created and restored by God's love in Jesus Christ. Such a vision gives us the freedom to pursue genetic research and yet opposes both manipulation of God's creation and any genetic stigmatising in human life. Chapter 5 continues this theological reflection in practical ways that many readers will find helpful. It examines the impact of human genetics on areas like marriage, work, insurance and pastoral care, and closes with a church member's moving testimony. The Report is offered to the Church and wider society as a starting point for further reflection and discussion.

Rev. Dr William Storrar, *Convener*
Rev. Dr Iain Torrance, *Secretary*
Study Group on Human Genetics, July 1995

HUMAN GENETICS
A Christian Perspective

The posing of moral and ethical questions by advances in science, technology and medicine is not a new phenomenon. Such advances have always posed questions about what is acceptable and right, and about what is unacceptable and wrong. Not only Christians ask these questions, but for Christians there are principles which govern our lives and our living which will make us approach the question in a different way and may ultimately lead to our reaching different conclusions. Frequently Christians have tried to find the answers to specific ethical problems in the Bible and in particular in the New Testament. The answer to specific questions and problems that face us in the modern world are not there – how could they be when the questions could not even have been imagined by the New Testament writers? But the Bible does give us general principles to follow in all areas of living, principally to recognise the worth of every individual, and the demand that we show to them the love Christ had for us.

The field of genetics is not the first medical field to pose difficult ethical questions for the Christian – human transplants and embryology are just two examples of areas where the Christian may be left confused and searching for guidance on what is ethically acceptable and what is not. But the field of genetics has received enormous media attention and has aroused speculation over a wide spectrum of society. The interest of some people is a general one, while others may have a more specific interest for they hope that advances in genetics may provide a cure for them or a loved one. What has taken most people by surprise, and has alarmed many people, is the speed with which developments are taking place. The changes are taking place so fast that only people working in the field are aware of the full impact of what is going on. It is sometimes difficult to believe how much has been achieved and

what may be achieved in the near future. With that background in mind it is clear that the ethical and moral questions that are posed are not static, but are changing all the time.

After considerable discussion, and following the advice of professional geneticists, the Board took the view that some extreme worries about possible genetic manipulation are without practical foundation. Although some developments might be theoretically possible, they appear most unlikely, because research and development is market driven, and similar ends may be achieved more cheaply. Deliberately taking a distinctive perspective, the Board tried to address recent genetic developments in the light of the theology of creation, and came to see the crucial ethical issue of genetic stigmatisation as being of paramount importance. This perspective echoes the line taken by the UNESCO International Bioethics Committee (as reported in *Nature*, Vol 371, 29 September 1994). This report maintains that 'debates about germline gene therapy, and "directed evolution", amount to much ado about nothing. The only application envisaged, namely, to spare descendants a serious disease, could ultimately be achieved more cheaply by sorting sperm or by selecting embryos'. Stigmatisation (ostracisation of individuals or groups for not meeting a genetic norm) is seen as the biggest threat from genome research. It is here that the Board believes the Church has a theology and a distinctive perspective to offer.

After an opening section introducing the reader to the terminology and science of human genetics (see also the Glossary, page 64), the book examines the possibilities and limits of genetic technology in the areas of genetic screening, testing and therapy. It then considers key aspects of the wider public debate on human genetics, particularly the contributions of the Government's Clothier and Nuffield Reports to the debate in Britain. The book then sets these issues within the distinctive theological perspective of the Church, offering a Trinitarian understanding of creation that establishes both the freedom and the limits of scientific, medical and social developments in the field of human genetics. This theological perspective then shapes the closing section of the report as it addresses a range of key issues for the Church and society; including the impact of human genetics on marriage,

' ... some extreme worries about possible genetic manipulation are without practical foundation.'

'The Board tried to address recent genetic develop-ments in the light of the theology of creation, and came to see the crucial ethical issue of genetic stigma-tisation as being of paramount importance.'

insurance, employment and attitudes to disability and genetic stigmatisation. The book is particularly concerned about the pastoral and practical responsibilities of the Church in response to these issues. Finally, the human dilemmas raised by genetics have been uppermost in the work of the Board and this is reflected in the report's epilogue which offers a moving account of personal and spiritual struggle with genetic illness. To help the reader, summaries of the argument are provided at key points in the book.

Chapter 2
A SCIENTIFIC PERSPECTIVE

The terminology and the ideas

Genes and the body

Our hearts, lungs, muscles, and most other parts of our body are bundles of cells. These cells, the building blocks, all have some features in common. They carry, as a rule, two copies of the 23 different **chromosomes** which are the bank of instructions (or **genetic information**) for making and operating the human body. One copy of each of the 23 has come from each parent. In total then each cell usually contains 46 chromosomes. The chromosomes are known by the numbers 1 to 22 (the **autosomes**), and the letters X and Y (the **sex chromosomes**).

Except for the sex chromosomes, the two members of any one pair of chromosomes are very similar to each other. Females also carry a pair of similar sex chromosomes, two X chromosomes. A male, however, has only one X chromosome, inherited from his mother, and a Y chromosome inherited from his father. The Y is quite different from the X. This means that apart from the instructions on a male's X chromosomes, we all have two sets of genetic instructions.

Each chromosome consists of a very long string of units of **DNA**, called nucleotides. There are four different nucleotides – A, T, C and G – and they are ordered in a unique sequence on each chromosome.

This unique sequence is read as a code. Subsections of the DNA sequence are read by a translation system as instructions for making particular **proteins**, the functional parts of the cell. Each cell carries all the genetic information, but different cells use different subsets of the information, and this causes the differences we see between heart, lung *etc.* The subset of the sequence coding for one protein is called a **gene**.

The DNA nucleotide sequence of the chromosomes is not unchanging and invariable. Consequently the 22 pairs of chromosomes which are similar – the autosomes – are not absolutely identical. While each of a pair usually carries the same selection of genes, the precise DNA sequence of a gene on one copy is often slightly different from the sequence on the other copy. These different versions of a gene are called **alleles**. This leads to individual differences which are either direct reflections of a difference in one gene, or else, when many gene products interact, to the precise mix of gene products. Thus some people have brown hair and some have red hair, due to a combination of slight differences in the alleles they carry in cells at the base of the hair which make the pigment proteins.

Individual differences are usually neutral: that is, they do not affect health in any noticeable way. However, some differences in the sequence of an allele are harmful. In these cases they lead to a change or loss of function of the product of that allele. If there is simply a loss of function, this does not necessarily affect the person who carries the allele, if it is on an autosomal chromosome, and only one of the pair carries the harmful allele. If both alleles are non-functional, however, this has a damaging effect on any parts of the body in which this particular gene is used. In the case of genes on the X chromosome, any male who carries a harmful allele will be affected, because he only has one copy of these genes. Where the different sequence of an allele leads not to loss but to changed and actively harmful function, a single copy of the allele, even in the presence of one normal allele, can have damaging effects. Such cases are known as autosomal dominant disorders, and one of the most common is Huntington's disease, which results in mental and physical deterioration in mid-adult life.

The current estimate is that there are in total about 100,000 genes on the chromosomes, of which perhaps 20–30,000 are used in each cell at some time. There are many cell types, and some of these genes are used in all of them. Others are just used in one or a few types of cell, and at particular times. For instance, Duchenne Muscular Dystrophy is caused by a harmful allele of a gene on the X chromosome, which is only used in muscle. Consequently only muscles are affected, and only in boys, since they have just one X chromosome.

Number of inherited diseases

There are currently estimated to be more than 4000 recorded inherited diseases which are caused by single genes. While most of these are very rare, several common cancers are often caused by harmful alleles which are carried by a substantial proportion of the population. The harmful effects are usually manifested in the middle or later years, and it is likely that any other common single gene disorders which are discovered in the future will tend to be late-acting.

In addition to different ages of onset, inherited diseases vary in their severity and in the ways they affect the individual. Among the most common are cystic fibrosis (CF), which affects about 1 in 2000 children born in Northern Europe, and Fragile X syndrome (Fra X) which affects 1 in 1400 boys. The second is X-linked. The worst effects of CF are on the lungs and occur after birth. In Fra X, the main effect is mental subnormality, and the damage starts during the early development of the brain, before birth. Although these are among the most common, they are still so rare that a general practitioner would probably only encounter one affected family during his career. Less common are, for instance, retinitis pigmentosa which causes deterioration of vision, and Marfan's syndrome which causes weaknesses in connective tissue, sometimes leading to heart failure in early adulthood.

Apart from disorders caused by single genes, there is evidence that combinations of particular alleles of several genes may increase the individual's susceptibility to conditions such as cancer and heart disease. Scientific knowledge is very incomplete in this area, and the effects on health usually appear to be marginal anyway.

Today's scientific and medical possibilities

Today the sequences corresponding to a number of human genes have been isolated, and every week another discovery is announced. DNA sequences from other species are also being isolated and characterised, including those of many harmful viruses and bacteria.

These sequences can be used in a number of ways. At present the main medical use is in diagnosis. In the case of the inherited diseases, the DNA sequence of a human gene can be used to diagnose much more precisely than any other method whether an individual is carrying one or more harmful alleles of the gene. An individual affected by cystic fibrosis will carry two harmful CF alleles. Their parents will each carry one harmful and one normal allele. In fact, 1 person in 20 in Northern Europe carries one harmful CF allele, but are unlikely to be aware of this unless they are married to a CF carrier and have had a CF child. At present, parents who have already had one CF child often seek foetal testing of later pregnancies, sometimes choosing to abort affected foetuses.

Changes can take place to alleles in a cell during the lifetime of an individual. In fact cancer and some other diseases are caused by such changes. Some of the genes associated with cancerous changes have now been isolated, and there is a possibility that they may be used to diagnose individuals at high risk of contracting particular cancers. This sort of diagnostic information may eventually be helpful in treatment and prevention of cancer.

Bacterial and viral sequences can be used to diagnose whether an individual is infected with them. This information can be used in the case of, for instance, a pregnant woman infected with cytomegalovirus, to support a decision to abort. They can also be used in the laboratory for developing vaccines and other therapeutic development.

Tomorrow's realistic possibilities

Screening

It would now be possible to screen (a) the whole population; (b) people known to be related to affected individuals, for a number of harmful alleles. This information could be used by the individuals to make choices about marriage partners, about whether to have a child, and whether to test foetuses. To screen the whole population would be extremely expensive, mainly because counselling is an essential accompaniment where the welfare of the individual is considered. However screening without counselling is offered in the United States of America by companies for some disorders, and will probably soon be available here on that basis, if the National Health Service does not offer it. In the United Kingdom, the NHS already undertakes widespread or population screening using non-genetic techniques for a number of disorders for which genetic factors have variable degrees of importance in aetiology, including phenylketonuria (PKU), spina bifida and Down's syndrome.

While it is theoretically possible that genetic screening could be used for many conditions, it is highly unlikely that it will be offered for most inherited disorders, because of their rarity and the vast expense which would then yield little returns in terms of improved health. This is even more discouraging to companies than to governments, since people are unwilling to pay for diagnostic services where they do not believe they are at significant risk. Consequently it is not worthwhile for profit making organisations to interest themselves in these areas.

Apart from affected families and their doctors, other people might use genetic information for their own purposes, for example insurance companies.

Gene therapy

Another possible use of the normal alleles of genes which cause the more common inherited diseases, and perhaps one day of some cancers, is in **gene therapy**. This involves delivering the normal Deoxyribose

'Consequently it is not worthwhile for profit making organisations to interest themselves in these areas.'

Nucleic Acid (DNA) sequence to cells of the affected tissues. Clinical trials of this technique have started in the USA, France and the UK. It is not expected that this approach will yield a cure, but that, for some diseases, it may be a significant addition to the therapeutic possibilities available. The technical difficulties are formidable, and because the treatment involves the introduction of material into the body, the developments must meet the rigorous regulatory demands imposed on drug development. Because of the vast resources required for each development, it is not likely that much work will be directed exclusively towards treatment of any but the commonest inherited disorders. However, since it is probable that the techniques may be useful for treatment of more common diseases such as cancer and respiratory diseases, work may be carried out using the inherited diseases as model systems. Thus it is difficult to predict how far gene therapy will be carried. Much will depend on just how successful the early experiments are, and whether ways of applying the knowledge in more common diseases can be found. Given the profit-orientation of companies and the tight control on health-care spending everywhere now, it seems likely that few possibilities will actually be pursued.

Gene therapy as described above involves treating only selected tissues, and does not include those which transmit genetic information to descendants. The possibility of applying gene therapy to embryos, so as permanently to alter the genetic constitution of an individual and its descendants, has been demonstrated successfully in animals. In the UK it has been ruled out of consideration on ethical grounds by the Clothier Committee. However, genetic testing of embryos and subsequent implantation of only those free from a genetic disease is another possibility which has already been used in the case of cystic fibrosis.

' ... it is not likely that much work will be directed exclusively towards treatment of any but the commonest inherited disorders.'

' ... genetic testing of embryos and subsequent implantation of only those free from a genetic disease is another possibility which has already been used in the case of cystic fibrosis.'

Summary

It is possible that more ethical problems will be posed by the improper use of genetic information by insurance companies and others, than by medical uses. One point of concern, however, might be worth mentioning. The growth of these testing possibilities puts some pressure on prospective parents to undergo increasing numbers of procedures, which may be of doubtful value. The individual can lose a sense of the biological normality of reproduction and feel excessive anxiety. If an affected child is born, there may be even more than the usual irrational guilt, just because there is a growing sense that the parents should and can control everything. Except for a few common conditions, such as CF, the likelihood of genetic testing yielding useful information is very small indeed, except where members of the immediate family are known to be affected. At present it is these affected families which are receiving testing services in the NHS, where suitable diagnostic sequences are available.

On the other hand, testing for non-inherited abnormal genetic conditions, such as the presence of dangerous viruses or extra chromosomes, may be of more general interest, although here again there are often issues of precisely when there is sufficient scientific and medical knowledge to justify the anxiety generated in the patient by the procedures. It is paradoxical that far more anxiety appears to have been generated by the information that a large number of cervical smear samples taken to screen healthy women for pre-cancerous changes have been mishandled in a way that might reduce the number of positive predictions made from them than would have been felt by the women concerned in the days before any test was available.

Limits of Genetic Technology?

Focusing the question

It is impossible to estimate the limits of what may become technologically possible. Who would have guessed ten years ago that we would have the technological capabilities we have now? Who can guess what new possibilities will be created in the next fifty years? All we can realistically hope to do is to consider the possibilities opened up by the technologies we have now, and how developments may be affected by, for example, resource constraints as well as those imposed by political choices.

The resource question will be extremely important, because basic research in this area is expensive and becoming steadily more so, while the development of a single therapeutic idea generated by this research into a new medical treatment involves vast expenditure. At present the cost of developing a new drug is around $300 million and becoming more expensive. A large part of this is due to testing through clinical trials; and now all new treatments, not just drugs, are being subjected to these lengthy and expensive evaluative procedures. This is part of a global trend towards establishing more cost-effective health-care which is unlikely to be reversed in the light of the high proportion of GDPs (Gross Domestic Product) already spent on health-care and the demand for proof of efficacy. One implication of this is that even where a particular health-care outcome is agreed to be desirable, if there are several technical ways of reaching this outcome, research and development of treatment are likely to focus speedily on the most cost-effective, generally acceptable approaches rather than spreading scarce resources over several approaches which have slightly different levels of public acceptability. Particularly if a therapeutic approach is likely to be much more expensive to develop or to administer, it is unlikely to obtain significant funding in competition with less demanding approaches.

The probable limits of current genetic technology

At present an increasing number of genetic probes are becoming available which are being used to explore the role of different genes, and different alleles of genes, in normal and pathological processes. By increasing understanding of the human body in sickness and health, this is adding to and refining the body of knowledge on which preventative and therapeutic medical decision-making is based. In addition, probes for the DNA of viruses which infect humans are being isolated and used in research and diagnosis. Thus genetic research is medically important through increasing understanding of both human genetics and the genetic characteristics of human pathogens.

Diagnostic testing

Some of these probes, which correspond to human genes which have alleles known to cause common, single gene disorders, are being used in diagnostic testing of individuals at risk of producing an affected child, and of foetuses which may be affected. Currently data derived by this means can be used by the couples involved to assist their reproductive decisions about whether to have a child, or in the case of an ongoing pregnancy, about whether to consider a termination. Better probes are constantly becoming available, and the statistical information they provide is becoming more precise. However as with all medical tests they will never be completely error-free.

At present, probes are only available for a few, relatively common single gene disorders. In time, probes for many of the rarer disorders will become available. In addition, probes are becoming available for genes for which it is believed that their different alleles may play a role in creating the differential individual risk of various common diseases, such as cancer. Here the quality of information yielded by testing at-risk individuals is going to be harder to assess, and for many conditions will be only minimally useful for predicting disease. How does one assess the value of the information where no treatment is available, for instance in breast cancer? In other cases, the information that an individual with the allele has a marginally higher expectation of death from, for example heart disease, 30 years after the test, is of doubtful use. On the other hand, in some cases like Marfan's syndrome, early diagnosis can be followed up with treatment to reduce the severity of the disease. However, the number of individuals for whom the use of genetic probes will yield clearly interesting and medically useful information for decision-making is almost certain to be quite small.

While diagnostic testing is highly acceptable to families with recessive disorders in which carriers are unaffected, a survey of individuals who were at 50:50 risk of developing Huntington's Chorea – a dominant disorder which develops in mid-adult life – found that approximately 50% did not want to know their own status, since if positive they would definitely develop the condition. Thus it is not easy to find a unified approach for dealing with all genetic disorders.

'Better probes are constantly becoming available ... as with all medical tests they will never be completely error-free.'

Population screening

Population screening for disorders using non-genetic techniques is long-established, *eg* screening new-borns for PKU and women for cervical pre-cancer. There is a possibility that **population-wide genetic screening** for carriers of cystic fibrosis, and perhaps other relatively common disorders, might be introduced in the UK where 1 in 20 of the population is a carrier. This would be carried out with the consent of the individual, informed by genetic counsellors. It would be extremely expensive, but there is considerable pressure from affected families. It has been suggested that it would be more cost-effective to screen for several disorders at the same time. This is a fallacy, since although the biochemical test for several would not cost significantly more than for one, most of the cost of screening is in the counselling. Since each disorder requires quite a different approach to pre-counselling, before the actual test, the pre-counselling session would become much more expensive, cancelling out savings on the biochemical tests.

Even if screening followed by termination of affected foetuses became universal for any recessive inherited disorder where carriers are unaffected, it would not significantly affect the frequency of these alleles in the population, since the majority of disease alleles are present in unaffected carriers rather than in affected individuals. Only for dominant disorders such as Huntington's disease would elimination of affected foetuses eventually reduce the allele in the population.

Population screening has also been suggested for HIV, although in the current state of public feeling and the high rate of false positives this is not likely to be introduced.

Gene therapy

Current attempts at somatic gene therapy aim to replace insufficient or absent gene function in specific, non-germline tissues. Gene therapy in general cannot repair damage to the body which has already taken place. Thus it is most likely to be attempted for disorders in which there is no significant prenatal damage.

Somatic gene therapy, involving the introduction of the DNA

coding for a defective or absent protein to cell populations whose function is seriously impaired by the defect, is currently being attempted for a small number of disorders including ADA (immune deficiency) and cystic fibrosis. Where regular administration of the extraneous DNA is possible, as in the lung epithelium of CF patients, there is no attempt to insert the extraneous DNA into the cells' own DNA, which would be more difficult and risky. In cases where the tissue is hard to reach, efforts are being made to insert the functional sequence in the target cells' DNA. Current research is trying to develop mini-chromosomes carrying extraneous genes which could be stably introduced into cells with less risk than insertional mutagenesis.

Gene therapy for acquired disorders

Another area of research is aimed at using gene therapy techniques to stop an abnormal process, rather than to replace a deficient function. This is looking at the possibility of removing unwanted sequences from some cells, such as viral or abnormally active endogenous sequences, or of blocking their activity in the cell. Some of these projects may offer viable ideas for future treatments further down the line, for cancerous conditions and for other diseases currently treated by conventional or biotechnological drugs.

In terms of their effects on the body, none of these interventions differs much from existing therapies, except in precision. CF gene therapy just goes one step further back than injecting insulin into a diabetic, whose cells have lost the ability to produce enough of this essential protein. The idea of using DNA to block pathological expression is not fundamentally different from using poisonous drugs to kill the affected cells, the current treatment for cancerous cells. Indeed, most biotechnological drugs now in use are proteins produced in culture from engineered human genes, such as insulin and tPA (for clotting and stroke). Using the artificially-synthesised and introduced DNA of such genes rather than the protein, would simply go one step back in the synthetic sequence.

Germline gene therapy

Changing the genes in human germ cells *might* become technically possible, but would be unattractive for a number of reasons. Technically it would be impossible to achieve anything close to 100% effectiveness, and thus in order to be acceptable there would still have to be one or more screening stages, probably at the post-fertilisation and foetal stages. Thus in the eyes of the several bodies (in the local hospital, in the Department of Health, and, soon, in the relevant European Union body) which have to give successive rounds of approval before each stage of a research programme involving human subjects, and in those of the bodies which provide resources for medical research and development, nothing would be gained over the currently feasible procedure of testing the foetus. To approve such research would neither be in accord with medical ethics nor economically attractive. Nor would it be attractive from the perspective of the scientist or clinician keen to advance his/her career, since the checks and balances in the system would indefinitely delay progress and the career progression of everyone involved in the development. Even if possible, it would be extraordinarily expensive to develop, and for all these reasons it is highly unlikely that attempts will be made to develop the technique. Even allowing for the unpredictability of technological advance, given the number of procedures that must be gone through to obtain the necessary approvals, we can feel confident that, at least for several years, germline gene therapy will not pose real ethical challenges. Consequently we do not consider it further at this time. However it should be noted that the currently feasible approaches, of aborting affected foetuses, and of implanting selected embryos, also have ethical implications.

Preimplantation embryo gene therapy

This might become technically possible, but again it would involve more steps, more risks and less likelihood of a positive outcome than *in vitro* fertilisation (IVF) followed by testing for normal embryos and implanting only these. This in its turn is much more expensive and failure prone than testing foetuses and abortion of abnormal foetuses, which is likely to be possible soon at very early stages of pregnancy and thus acceptable to a high proportion of couples.

Resource implications

Given the limitations on scientific and financial resources, it is unlikely that more than a few of the possibilities opened up by the techniques noted above will be developed into usable treatments, even for the rich.

Informational implications

While superficially it would appear that the gene probes becoming available offer a great deal of relevant information about individuals, in fact because the genes' effects on bodily function are the result of a complex interplay between many genes and the environment, only a few probes, not all human, really pose a problem. HIV test results are a clear case of this.

How is gene therapy breaking new ground?

'*Plus ça change, plus c'est la même chose*'. The main impact of the new technology will be on the body of knowledge about normal and abnormal human bodily functions. It is probable that resource limitations will block the more contentious and novel treatment developments rather than moral concerns. It is important to remember also that any influential group can influence the allocation of these scarce resources towards the most acceptable applications, determined by whatever seem the most important criteria.

Perhaps the question is not only whether these applications offer new moral problems, but whether, even where they are judged to be morally acceptable, they merit the resources they will consume. The choice may be between on the one hand genetic screening or better therapy for rare conditions such as CF, and on the other hand more care in the community for old people.

Risk factors

It must be borne in mind that all medical interventions have some associated risk of harmful outcomes, and in general the utility of a procedure including administration of drugs is assessed by taking this into account, on the basis of estimated balance of benefits. Risks include human error, which is impossible to banish completely, but also inherent risks of the treatment or drug, such as occasional side effects. While it is becoming usual to explain the risks and their probability to patients, there is no certainty that the patient will understand the explanation. It is clear that most people find it difficult to understand the significance of a statement of probability, and this is of particular importance for genetic counselling where the risks are often presented as quite complex statements of probable outcomes.

An example: CF and the choices

Cystic fibrosis is one of the most common single gene inherited defects in Northern Europe and the USA, affecting between 1 in 2000 and 1 in 2500 births. It results when an individual has two abnormal copies of the CF gene and lacks the function provided by normal genes. Most individuals have two normal copies of the gene; carriers have one normal and one defective copy and the normal copy is sufficient for them to function normally. While 1 in 20 of the North European population carries one abnormal copy of the CF gene, only when both parents are carriers is there a 1 in 4 risk of having an affected child.

At present people usually discover this risk when they have their first CF child. Most of the damage done by CF occurs after birth, is cumulative, but is being treated with increasing success. However, affected individuals still usually die before the age of 30. Somatic gene therapy may improve the situation, but will not be a cure. In the UK parents who are carriers can then make the following reproductive choices:

1   They can avoid future pregnancies.
2   They can undergo diagnostic testing of themselves and, using amniocentesis, of their unborn child. This can show with increasing reliability (but not 100%) whether the foetus is affected. If it is, they can choose to terminate or not.

In theory they could undergo *in vitro* fertilisation (IVF), selecting (almost certainly) unaffected embryos, but this carries some risks and is not highly successful. It is also expensive and availability is limited on the NHS.

Somatic CF Gene Therapy

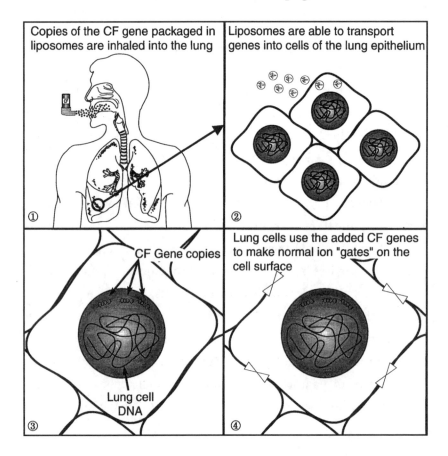

① Copies of the CF gene packaged in liposomes are inhaled into the lung

② Liposomes are able to transport genes into cells of the lung epithelium

③ CF Gene copies
Lung cell DNA

④ Lung cells use the added CF genes to make normal ion "gates" on the cell surface

More information on CF and comparison with Fragile X

Cystic Fibrosis

Cystic fibrosis affects a number of tissues. The most seriously affected organ is the lung, which undergoes progressive deterioration leading to premature death. While understanding of the biochemical mechanisms was limited until after the discovery of the gene in 1989, extensive research on the disease process led to the realisation that the main damage to the lung was a secondary effect caused by the multiple infections suffered by affected individuals in whom the lung secretions were excessively thick and failed to clear. This awareness allowed great improvements in management of the disease by antibiotics and physiotherapy. Appreciation that the efficiency of digestion is also impaired has led to improvements in general health through special nutritional measures.

The isolation of a number of related probes, and finally the gene itself in 1989, has provided probes which can now accurately detect 85% of carriers in the population. A number of centres have just completed, or are currently running, clinical trials of population screening for CF, supported by the Cystic Fibrosis Research Trust, the Government's Medical Research Council (MRC) and the Wellcome Foundation (a charitable Trust). These include surveys of patient, family and general public attitudes towards screening which have been found to be generally favourable, particularly among affected groups . At present, genetic tests are mainly carried out on members of families known to have produced affected individuals to determine the likelihood that a couple will produce an affected child. Prenatal diagnostic testing of at-risk foetuses is also carried out where the prospective parent wishes to terminate a pregnancy which would produce an affected child.

Development of gene therapy has advanced to the stage of phase 1 clinical trials (which are designed to determine safety in human use, but do not assess efficacy). A total of six independent trials in the USA and UK had been approved and three in UK and France were awaiting approval in November 1989. Most of these are now approved and in progress. While these are designed to test for safety, some evidence of short-lasting effect has already been obtained in one case. All experiments so far are aimed at treating the lung, although some have started with the nose. Even if this achieves success, many more technical hurdles will have to be overcome to treat less accessible parts of the body.

At this point the MRC has set up several Centres for Gene Therapy in the UK. One of these is for CF and is led from Edinburgh. This has ensured another tranche of development funding for somatic gene therapy – about £5 million – but this is not nearly sufficient to carry even one development through to final approval for wider use.

The Cystic Fibrosis Research Trust was founded in London in 1964 by a group of parents of affected children. Its main objectives are to raise funds to finance research to find a cure for CF, and to improve the care and treatment of people with CF. It also aims to provide support and advice to affected families and to educate the public about CF. It has so far funded more than £15 million of research. Its sister charities in other countries have also, on occasion, funded research in the UK.

The Fragile X Syndrome

This syndrome acquired its name from the appearance of the X chromosomes carrying the affected sequence, when cells of affected individuals were cultured under defined conditions. The affected X chromosome often appeared to break or hang by a thin thread at a specific site along its length. This characteristic was for a time the main diagnostic test.

In contrast with CF, the most obvious effects of Fragile X are on the mind rather than the body. It is the single most common cause of mental retardation after Down's syndrome. The degree to which individuals with an affected X chromosome show mental retardation is variable. The incidence of the syndrome is approximately 1 in 1400 in boys and 1 in 2100 for girls (female carriers, who have a normal X in addition to the Fragile X, are less often and less severely affected). Affected individuals do have some physical abnormalities. They tend to have long faces and everted ears (mis-shapen), but these are not striking to the untrained eye. The degree of mental retardation in males is variable, with symptoms ranging from moderate learning difficulties in some individuals to severe handicap in others.

Awareness of the syndrome, and diagnosis rates, have been low in general and very variable between regions, although some in the UK and elsewhere have offered diagnosis since the mid 1980s. Treatment possibilities for the main problem – mental handicap – have been limited. Special educational programmes and a variety of medications have been used but with modest effect.

The associated gene was isolated in 1991 and this has provided a tool to study the abnormal developmental process of the syndrome, which was completely mysterious, as well as to improve diagnosis. While there is still no information about the processes affected, ongoing studies of gene expression suggest that the gene is significantly more active in the central nervous system (CNS) and testes than in other tissues, and that expression is present in normal adult tissue. Earlier behavioural studies report mental subnormality from an early age, but there is evidence to suggest a further significant decline in IQ throughout. This suggests damage to the unborn child may be important, but postnatal therapy might also limit the deterioration. This would only be the case provided that deterioration is due to the action of the gene. The alternative possibility is that the early established abnormalities lead to a reduction of the child's ability to interact effectively with the environment, and thus to a progressive failure to learn.

The Fragile X Society was founded in November 1989 by a group of parents whose children had been diagnosed as affected by the syndrome. They contacted all interested professionals known to them. Their aims at this point are to provide support and information to families, raise public and professional awareness and encourage research. At present, a very high proportion of inquiries are from professionals looking for more information about the syndrome. The Department of Health awarded a capital grant to help establish a database of families in 1992. The relatively recent date of formation of the Society is due in part to low awareness of the syndrome and consequent low rate of diagnosis in many regions. Another suggested reason is the social stigma attached to mental retardation which may have discouraged families from seeking a high profile for the condition in the past.

Significant differences between CF and Fragile X

CF and Fragile X are similar in their general incidence in the population, they are both costly to society, and the genes are now available for use in further research, as well as for diagnosis and therapy. However, there are several major differences between their phenotypic expression which have had considerable importance for progress towards improvements in therapy. These fall into two categories: *technical differences* and *sociological differences*.

Technical differences

CF	Fragile X
1 Knowledge of the site of expression and mode of action of the CF gene is well-advanced.	1 Very little is known about the action of the Fragile X gene.
2 The worst-affected tissue is the lung. There is an extensive body of expertise in delivering therapeutic agents to the lung.	2 The worst-affected tissue is in the CNS. The science of delivering agents to any or all parts of the brain is in its infancy.
3 While there is prenatal damage to the pancreas, damage to the lung starts after birth and follows a slow progression. Thus treatment of the lung has the possibility of making a major impact.	3 Intervention would probably have to be at an early stage in prenatal development to be effective.
4 Avoidance through abortion.	4 Avoidance through abortion possible.
5 Treatments of increasing effectiveness available.	5 Prospect of effective treatment doubtful.

Sociological differences

CF	Fragile X
1 There is a high degree of public awareness.	1 Public and professional awareness are still low.
2 Families have formed a powerful and sophisticated pressure group through the Trust. Little stigma attached to manifestations of syndrome.	2 No strong pressure group. Stigma attached to mental handicap may inhibit development.
3 Hopes generated by scientific success with clear therapeutic possibilities.	3 While some hopes have been generated, there is not, as yet, enough knowledge of gene action, and gene therapy to formulate therapeutic ideas.

Summary

We cannot predict what possibilities new technology might open up in the future. However, we can be reasonably confident that new treatments and products will not be sprung on us without many years of warning. The development of any new treatment or medical product is a very slow and costly process, particularly when there is public recognition that there are complex ethical questions to resolve. Those which are already under development, *ie* somatic gene therapy for various disorders, will not be generally available for at least five years, even if there are no set-backs in the development process.

As CF and Fragile X show, the technical and human problems differ between different inherited disorders. Consequently each condition poses a new set of challenges, and addressing each of these demands considerable resources. In the foreseeable future, with probable continuing constraints on health-care and research expenditure, the development of the possibilities of treating many rare conditions with

' ... new treatments and products will not be sprung on us without many years of warning. The development of any new treatment or medical product is a very slow and costly process.'

' ... each condition poses a new set of challenges.'

novel genetic techniques is likely to be limited. Decision-makers in the Department of Health will be loath to expend scarce resources on new developments where facilities which they regard as satisfactory are already available: *eg* they will favour the existing techniques of abortion of affected foetuses or implantation of selected embryos over embarking on a new programme of development.

The situation is rather different for diagnostic testing, which is now available for a growing number of conditions. Here there are definite problems about the possible abuse of such information, and whether diagnosis should be attempted where no treatment is available.

Chapter 3
A PUBLIC
and ETHICAL PERSPECTIVE

Aspects of the wider debate on Human Genetics

During the 1970s and 1980s there has been greater awareness and anxiety over the health and environmental consequences of the new technologies. This has led to the formulation of more rigorous standards for the assessment of new processes and has stimulated a widescale public debate. This has taken place at the level of national governments, international conventions (which have brought about a convergence of the laws and guidelines in the industrialised countries), church groups and the press. For example, in the United Kingdom, the health and safety aspects of work which involve genetic modification are controlled by the Health and Safety at Work Act (1974). This is administered by the Health and Safety Executive (HSE). Employers are legally obliged to inform the HSE of work involving genetic modification and to conduct a risk assessment. The Genetic Manipulation Advisory Group (GMAG), later the Advisory Committee on Genetic Modification (ACGM), advises the HSE on risk assessment.

The ACGM, through the production of guide-lines, has been crucial in developing regulation in the UK. Within the European Community, a number of directives on genetic questions have to be implemented into the national law of member states. An ecumenical group, on which the Church of Scotland's Society, Religion and Technology Project (SRT) is represented, is in dialogue with a committee of the Council of Europe on the terms and articles of the draft Bioethics Convention (Convention for the Protection of Human Rights and Dignity of the Human Being with Regard to the Application of Biology and Medicine). The World Council of Churches produced a report *Biotechnology: Its Challenges to the Churches and the World* in August 1989. There have been numerous local and denominational reports and conferences.

Aspects of the public debate in Britain

The Clothier and Nuffield Reports

In November 1989 the Government set up the Committee on the Ethics of Gene Therapy under the chairmanship of Sir Cecil Clothier. In January 1992 it produced the *Report of the Committee on the Ethics of Gene Therapy* ('The Clothier Report'). Among its main conclusions and recommendations, the Committee recommended 'that somatic cell gene therapy should, for the present, be conducted according to the discipline of research and governed by the exacting requirements which already apply in the United Kingdom to research involving human subjects' (chapter 8.5). The Committee found that 'Somatic cell gene therapy will be a new kind of treatment, but it does not represent a major departure from established practice, nor does it, in our view, pose new ethical challenges' (chapter 8.8). However, on the issue of germ line gene therapy, the Committee reported: 'we have concluded that there is insufficient knowledge to evaluate the risks to future generations. We recommend, therefore, that gene modification of the germ line should not yet be attempted.'

Emeritus Professor Margaret Stacey (formerly Professor of

Sociology at the University of Warwick) was one of those invited by the subsequent Nuffield Committee to respond to its Report at the public Conference the Committee organised in London in March 1994. She also submitted comments on the Clothier Report. These comments were unpublished, but she supplied a copy to the Board of Social Responsibility Study Group, and gave permission for the Board to refer to them.

Professor Stacey warned: 'The social and cultural changes which may result from gene therapy have been ignored by the Committee. Consequently consideration of a range of ethical issues is omitted. In chapter 3 there is recognition that attitudes in future may change (3.2). However, there is no overt recognition that the introduction of genetic manipulation will itself inevitably change perceptions and beliefs about what it is proper for individuals to ask others to do to them or their children .... The very concept of what it is to be a human being has already begun to be changed by prenatal diagnosis.'

She comments that: ' ... changes which may be wrought in beliefs and values are not referred to. Much innovative practice in human reproduction has already changed social values. The introduction of prenatal tests has modified expectations about childbirth and placed new responsibilities on mothers to avoid the delivery of an impaired neonate .... The new definitions required for parenthood embodied in the Human Fertilisation and Embryology Act show how far assisted reproduction has already changed social reality. Such changes have wider social and cultural consequences than for the relatively few infertile women and men to whom the procedures are applied ....'

As we have seen, it was the finding of the Clothier Committee that somatic cell gene therapy will be a new kind of treatment, but, in their view, 'it does not represent a major departure from established medical practice', nor does it 'pose new ethical challenges'.

Professor Stacey commented: 'Given the failure to examine the entire social and cultural area the claim that no new ethical principles are involved cannot be made. There is social science evidence to suggest that the use of prenatal diagnosis has changed a woman's experience of pregnancy and initiated social and cultural changes about the meaning of motherhood, the acceptability of impaired children and

'The introduction of prenatal tests has modified expectations about childbirth and placed new responsibilities on mothers to avoid the delivery of an impaired neonate.'

' ... the use of prenatal diagnosis has changed a woman's experience of pregnancy.'

adults. What the implication of these changes in the longer run may be has yet to be established; not all may be benign ....'

Professor Stacey concluded 'that the only conditions under which gene therapy could be permitted to proceed would be under carefully controlled conditions ... social and cultural conditions must be satisfied as well as medical ones'. She recommended 'that the regulatory body should include social scientists as well as medical scientists and social workers or counsellors as well as medical practitioners. It should also include persons who have genetic disorders and members of ethnic minorities. At least half the committee should be composed of women, given the burden of treatment they would bear in the case of manipulation of embryos and also for the care of the impaired'.

The **Nuffield Council on Bioethics** was set up in 1991 to consider the ethical issues provoked by the advances in biomedical research. It focused on the question of genetic screening for its first report, and in December 1993 it produced an excellent, authoritative and careful document entitled: *Genetic Screening: Ethical Issues*. It is worth reporting in some detail the range and conclusions of this report, before developing certain particular lines of criticism and comment. It addresses the crucial initial questions of consent and confidentiality.

The **Nuffield Report** identified four initial issues in the area of genetic screening:

1   There may be a wide margin of error in assessing the risks affecting individuals and families.
2   The results of screening may raise issues of such importance for a family that it might well become difficult to apply the established principles of confidentiality between a physician and an individual patient.
3   A satisfactorily ethical handling of the new information yielded by screening might make considerable demands on professional and health resources (this brings in questions of *appropriate* counselling and *informed* consent).
4   There is a danger of possible eugenic abuse.

The Report saw the need to create a broad framework of public understanding, in which the issues of proper consent, confidentiality and monitoring could be located.

In this identification of issues, we would highlight two aspects in particular: genetic knowledge is unusual, in that the information it provides seeps from one person to others (and it is this which raises different questions about confidentiality and what constitutes adequate – or informed – consent); and this knowledge (like any knowledge) is not simply a matter of 'cut and dried fact' which may be absorbed and assented to purely rationally, but requires a social context within which it is perceived as knowledge, and accepted and put to use. It is such a context which the Report calls for, by means of increased public awareness and education in genetics.

After an account of what genes are, and a description of current (1993) programmes of genetic screening, the Nuffield Report addresses the questions of providing information and obtaining consent (chapter 4). That is, it considers the information it considers people need to decide whether or not to accept screening, and the meaning and the implications of 'informed consent'. It notes that consenting to screening is different from consenting to treatment. With treatment, the individual initiates the process (seeks help). With screening, there is a process initiated (offered) by some other agent, to an individual who is apparently 'well'. Consenting to screening is different from consenting to treatment, as families are implicated when genetic information is discovered. These family members may not be in close touch, and may not have given consent to being screened. Informed consent also involves facing and thinking through unintended consequences: possibly protracted therapy; possibly termination of a pregnancy; possibly avoiding having further children. It is also the case that a test result may give no certain prediction, but a range of possibilities which have to be assessed.

To make a beginning, the Nuffield Report quotes the Department of Health's 1990 circular, *A Guide to Consent for Examination or Treatment*. This stipulates that patients are entitled to receive *sufficient* information to understand the proposed treatment, the possible *alternatives*, and the *risks*. Patients must be allowed to decide whether they will agree to the treatment, and they may refuse or withdraw consent at any time (Report, p 31; Department of Health, NHS Management Executive, undated, chapter 1, paragraph 2). Building on this, the Report suggests that the kinds of information a person needs before consenting to being screened include:

1   How serious is the genetic condition which may be disclosed?
2   How variable are its effects?
3   What are the therapeutic options?
4   How is the disorder transmitted (dominant, recessive)?
5   What is the significance of being a carrier?
6   What is the reliability of the screening test?
7   The fact that screening may reveal unwanted information (paternity).

The implication of the Report, understandably enough, is that if one can provide this, one is providing *sufficient* information for *informed* consent. It allows that especially difficult questions emerge with the identification of late onset diseases like Huntington's disease or Alzheimer's disease. Is abortion an acceptable option when the probability of a late onset disease is identified? The Report notes that future screening programmes will have to provide a more precise understanding of 'late onset', and the implication is that this will then give sufficient information for informed consent. Our concern, as the Church, is to try to address these dilemmas at a more fundamental level. Information may only be received and make sense within a specific context. Within what context (culture) then will such information (of late onset disease, carrier status, *etc*) make sense? How does a specifically Christian culture receive *this* kind of news? How does the possibility of being a carrier affect our self-understanding? Are we the kind of community which can give a welcome to the non-standard or disabled? Are we the kind of community which will reject those who will later develop disease? Such issues force the Church to ask what kind of community it is, and what is the understanding of hope which it brings to the world.

The Report underlines the importance of avoiding any hint of

'Are we the kind of community which can give a welcome to the non-standard or disabled? Are we the kind of community which will reject those who will later develop disease? Such issues force the Church to ask what kind of community it is, and what is the understanding of hope which it brings to the world.'

coercion in genetic screening programmes (p 34). It notes (p 35) that a review of routine screening for Down's syndrome in antenatal care indicated that the information provided was 'often not adequate and that women are not always sure of what tests they have undergone or what the results mean'.

The Report notes that in most pilot projects, written information has been supplemented by counselling. But, drawing on the results of two London trials to introduce genetic screening, it noted how difficult it was to convey adequate information to people who did not perceive a need for the knowledge that the test would supply (p 36). It maintains that genetic matters are complex, but 'can be explained … by means of written material plus a brief discussion' (p 36). It notes that counselling should be 'non-directive', but admits that in practice a dialogue which helps an individual is 'unlikely to remain completely neutral'. It suggests that counselling should include stress on: the voluntary nature of the screening, and the freedom and responsibility of the individual to decide; the importance of ensuring that the individual understands the purpose of the test and the significance of a positive result; an assurance of confidentiality coupled with a stress on the responsibility of individuals to inform partners and family members; an emphasis, at each stage, that consent to screening does not imply consent to any specific treatment or to the termination of a pregnancy. The Report also offers careful consideration of procedures to be adopted when attempting to gain informed consent from minors and the mentally ill or those with severe learning difficulties.

All of this chapter of the Nuffield Report is careful and conscientious. We note how it struggles to define adequate information, and to quantify it. We would suggest that part of the Report's difficulty is in thinking that 'information' is neutral, and that if you give enough information of the right kind, you reach 'adequacy'. Building on the Nuffield Report, we would suggest that one cannot bring about *consent* without producing *commitment*, and that one cannot produce commitment without arousing the *will*. The will is partially fuelled on 'fact' (physical data, statistics), but only partially. The Nuffield Report is right to stress the 'factual' side, as any responsible authority must endeavour to be truthful. But the will is also fuelled by *vision* (a creative, integrating understanding of how everything hangs together), which cannot be quantified. It would follow that we would want to suggest that 'adequacy' of information is not just a matter of quantity, but also of vision: it is information located within a context which has the power to sway the will.

The question then arises, with these new genetic questions, of the nature of the vision with which the statistics are received. As the Church, the community of those who respond to the self-giving life, death and resurrection of Christ, we have a distinctive and costly social vision. This must include a commitment to the vulnerable and the weak. Faced with new questions, new responsibilities and new dilemmas, the Church must re-examine its self-understanding. Is it really a community formed by the costly love of Christ?

The Church must be concerned not just with information and statistics, but with the impact on and consequences for the whole person when it considers the reception of any genetic/screening information. It must unleash its imagination to think of new ways of supporting those who are most in need. Our vision differs from that of Nuffield. A practical instance of this is the Board of Social Responsibility's new unit for severely disabled children at Springburn in Glasgow, called The Mallard.

We turn to the way the Nuffield Report addresses the question of the results of genetic screening and the issues these raise for confidentiality (chapter 5 of the Report).

The Report suggests that after screening, an individual should normally be fully informed of the result. There may be difficulties, if screening produces results which are unwanted, unexpected and not covered by previous consent.

However, the Report sees more intractable difficulties where the screening of an individual produces results which seriously affect the interest of others. It notes that the perceived interests of members of the same family may sometimes clash. The writers of the Report reviewed existing case law, professional guidelines and current academic writing of the application of the principle of confidentiality where information arises which might be vital to the well-being or future of other family members (p 43). The Report noted that 'in such clearly defined

'As the Church ... we have a distinctive and costly social vision. This must include a commitment to the vulnerable and the weak.'

page 33

contexts, it may be appropriate to treat those family members as a "unit" and to place less emphasis on individual patient autonomy' (p 43). This is an interesting comment, to which we will return later.

However, the approach taken to the problem by the Report is along more traditional lines. It allows that the accepted standards of confidentiality should be followed as far as possible. Where the application of such standards would result in grave damage to others, it suggests the health professionals should seek to persuade the individual to disclose the information. The Report opens the idea that in exceptional cases, health professionals might be justified in disclosing genetic information to other family members, against the individual's wish. To cover such cases, the Report recommends that the appropriate professional bodies prepare guidelines (p 53).

On what basis is this conclusion reached? The Report quotes Article 8(1) of the European Convention on Human Rights, which upholds the right of everyone to privacy in home, family life and correspondence (p 44). The Report allows that there may be disagreement about the extent to which privacy is to be protected, but concedes that there is such a thing as privacy. Yet it goes on to refer to Article 8(2) of the European Convention, which provides that the individual's right to personal privacy may be overridden by legally introduced requirements to protect health or morals or the rights and freedoms of others (p 45). Thus the Report acknowledges that a claim to privacy is not absolute. Others may claim to have a legitimate interest. The strength of that claim will vary: A relative for whom non-disclosure might lead to an unnecessary termination has a different claim from a query as to whether a prospective partner is likely in the long term to suffer from breast cancer (p 45).

Similarly, the Report shows how confidentiality is protected by common law principles; the Data Protection Act 1984; and professional rules of conduct (the General Medical Council's guidelines). Yet none of these defend a confidentiality which is absolute: each provides for confidentiality to the individual to be overridden in exceptional cases where disclosure is in the public interest, or to prevent injury or other damage to the health of any person or persons.

Having established both that confidentiality is important and that it may be breached, the Report addresses the question of how to broker the exceptional cases. Against the suggestion that there be created a legally enforceable duty on the part of the individual to disclose information, or that doctors should be placed under a legal duty to reveal information, the Report attempts to develop the notion of the responsibility of the individual (p 49): 'We adopt the view that a person acting responsibly would normally wish to communicate important genetic information to other family members.'

The Report allows that, exceptionally, an individual may withhold information from malice. Here it accepts that the individual's wishes may properly be overridden by a doctor (p 50), and it recommends that professional bodies prepare guidelines (p 53).

The Question of Confidentiality

How are people to comment on this handling of the question of confidentiality? In the previous chapter on adequate information to produce informed consent, we suggested that the Report relied too much on a model of rationality alone. In this chapter, dealing with the issue of confidentiality, we suggest the Report over relies on a model of private individualism.

It begins by noting the complexity of confidentiality, where others than the individual screened may have a legitimate interest in the result. But what is the understanding of humanity, the framework, within which this question is complex? If you begin with a hard, post-Enlightenment understanding of the individual, then confidentiality will either be absolute (a basically Kantian stance), or up for utilitarian grabs (a basically Millian stance).

If people are to take genetic information seriously, it may be that the Churches can help us to unclench from individualism and have a different vision. We suggest that the discovery of genetic knowledge invites us, at least at certain levels, to unpick post-Enlightenment individualism. People are not such separate, isolated persons as they thought. This in turn leads to another question:

What kind of a society are we that genetic information should be

'What kind of
society are we that
genetic information
should be
perceived as such
a threat that we
might want to hug it
to ourselves?
Are there alternative
ways in which
personhood may
be protected, not
by rules of privacy,
but by a common
vision of respect
and mutual
interdependence
and help?'

perceived as such a threat that we might want to hug it to ourselves? Are there alternative ways in which personhood may be protected, not by rules of privacy, but by a common vision of respect and mutual interdependence and help?

This is to build upon the instinct of the Report noted above, that it may be appropriate to treat family members as a 'unit', placing less emphasis on individual patient autonomy (p 43). Having painted itself into a corner defending individualism, the Report attempts to extricate itself by appealing to the individual's sense of responsibility. It is not clear that this argument will work. Such a sharply defined individualism is not other-directed. By beginning where it does, the Report does not have a grammar which will lead it out of the problem it identifies: it has no bridge to lead it into the social solidarity it sees as a solution. By starting in a different place, and offering a different vision of community and the inter-relatedness of people, which comes from our worship of the Trinitarian God, the Church may be able to show the way toward a more hospitable and responsive reception of genetic information, because we are committed to providing a context in which persons are genuinely valued and we are less afraid of others.

Chapter 8 of the Report addresses a third major ethical issue: the fear that genetic screening will lead to the *stigmatisation* of non-standard individuals. Stigmatisation is defined as 'branding, marking, or discrediting because of a particular characteristic' (p 77). The stigmatisation of individuals is linked to **eugenics**: the belief 'that it is possible and desirable, through selective breeding and the elimination of undesirable individuals, to alter the hereditary qualities of a race or population' (p 79).

The Report allows that 'there have always been some negative social reactions to disability in all its forms ' (p 77). It goes on, somewhat helplessly, to point to a paradox in our modern society: on the one hand an effort is made 'to create an environment in which people with a disability are accepted into society and seen as having a worthwhile life'; on the other hand 'resources are spent on preventing their births'. It cites the fear that an emphasis on the genetic differences between ethnic groups could increase social discrimination (racism).

What may be done to avoid this? The Report may be aware of its vulnerability on this score. It suggests that proper educational programmes should reduce these dangers. 'A well-informed individual is less likely to feel stigmatised than a poorly-informed individual who has received little or no counselling' (p 79). It continues, more effectively, 'it could be argued that, if we all found out our genetic variations, then there would be less concern about stigma'. Its major conclusion is that as a safeguard against eugenic abuse, the Report's recommendations on 'adequately informed consent, confidentiality and the central coordination and monitoring of genetic screening programmes' should be implemented (p 81).

May we, as the Church, take this any further? We would suggest that stigmatisation is the downside of the celebration of rationalistic individualism. On that model of human action and society, it would be almost impossible to avoid (we tend to define ourselves by vilifying others).

Are there any other possibilities? If we have genetic knowledge (and we do), must we inevitably have stigmatisation, racism and eugenics? One line of response would be to confine genetic screening and engineering to the therapy of *serious* illnesses. A difficulty here is how to take account of the extent to which illnesses are socially constructed (as Margaret Stacey has reminded us). Another line of response would be to acknowledge more wholeheartedly the extent to which 'disability' is a social construct (Margaret Stacey tells us: 'What is disabling varies from one society to another depending on the nature of the society', in her comments on the *Report of the Committee on the Ethics of Gene Therapy*). There are cultures which prize sameness (all males over six foot, blond and blue-eyed). There are other cultures which glory in variety. Similarly, what is considered responsible, even what is considered expensive (in terms of the consumption of time and money), are socially defined. If genetic knowledge, rather than making us more competitive (possessive of the knowledge of 'our' genes), can teach us that we are more inter-dependent than we thought, we will all gain from it. This may be another avenue in which the Churches can take the lead.

We have spoken of a 'socially defined' reality. Can this be put more theologically? What is the specific context out of which the Church sees the world and developments in genetic science (and other sciences)? We suggest that the Church has an understanding of creation which is distinctive: it both insists that we draw limits, and yet may genuinely welcome new developments. Christian understanding of creation cannot be separated from our understanding of God as Trinity. In this we have a vision which permits us to receive what is genuinely new in its possibilities (genetic information), but yet to possess this within a framework which will lead the Church always to summon the world to responsible stewardship, and away from manipulation, greed, and short-sighted objectives. When faced with the new, we need a recovery of theological vision, not to retreat into our shells.

Chapter 4
A THEOLOGICAL PERSPECTIVE

The Trinitarian basis of Creation

Let us begin by thinking about the doctrine of God, especially within a Reformed perspective. We will look at the two *new* acts of God in creation and incarnation, tracing their movement and implications. The doctrine of the Trinity, of course, is presupposed by the doctrine of the incarnation, but we will suggest that as we trace out the trajectory of the incarnation, our understanding of the Trinity is immeasurably enriched, and that this in turn feeds into a deeper understanding of creation. At the same time, this deepening understanding of incarnation enriches our understanding of creation to such an extent that we shall suggest the two doctrines may be drawn together, enriching and illuminating each other, like two binocular lenses. Finally, as we bring the two doctrines together, we shall suggest that through both of them we see flowing a single adaptive movement of the Trinitarian love of God, which leads to a Christian doctrine of personhood and community rather than a narrow individualistic world view.

How do we understand God? Reformed theology has learned the lesson of Karl Barth that we have no neutral or abstract or anthropomorphic access to God. We may only know God through his own self-disclosure. Hence, we may only *think* of God in terms of what he *does,* for *who* God *is* is no different from what he *does.* God's being is the same as his act: it is impossible for God to be inconsistent with himself.

How then do we understand the *act* of God, perhaps thinking specifically of his creativity, his acts of creative power? If we turn to the creed, we confess that we believe in one God, *the Father Almighty, Maker of heaven and earth.* This description of God, that he is almighty, is significantly brought into connection with the expression that he is Father. 'The one word explains the other; the Father is almightiness and almightiness is the Father' (Karl Barth: *Dogmatics in Outline,* London, 1949, p 46). It follows from this that we reject any and all impersonal notions of divine omnipotence, because sheer omnipotence as an abstract concept is arbitrary and demonic. We may only think in terms of who God *actually is*, and what God *actually does*.

It is similar when we speak of God as Father. When we dare to do this, we do so not in a neutral or abstract or anthropomorphic sense, but we mean that he is the God and Father of our Lord Jesus Christ. We do not, and cannot, know God as Father in himself, or as *our* Father, *apart from* his only Son Jesus Christ, in whom, and through the Holy Spirit, God gives us access to himself.

It follows that we know God in his nature when our knowledge of him is controlled by Jesus Christ. It follows further that we have no knowledge of *the power* of God except through Christ. At Matthew 28:18, it is Jesus who says: 'All power is given unto me in heaven and on earth.' God's almightiness 'becomes visible and alive *as saving and righteous power*' (Barth, p 49).

As Jesus Christ is the only-begotten Son of the Father, he is the *only* way God makes himself known as the Father. It is here that we see the *exclusiveness* of the revelation in Christ, through the Spirit, both of the Father and of the almightiness of God. Since the Father is never without the Son and the Spirit, all that the Father *does* is done in, through, and with, the Son and the Spirit. This is the only God we know.

An enormously significant point is related to this. While God is always Father, he was neither always creator nor always incarnate.

This means that the creation of the world out of nothing is something new even for God. God was always Father, but he *became* creator. It is an astonishing act, and it is in a similar way that we must think of the **incarnation**, for although God was always able to become incarnate, we are told that he chose to do this in 'the fullness of time' (Galatians 4:4).

So what we see are two radically new acts: the creation and the incarnation. Both issue from the Holy Trinity. What we want to do is explore each in turn, to see how they are related to the Holy Trinity and to each other, and how they lead to a realisation of inter-relatedness and interdependence in humanity. We are created for relationship with God and one another.

First, in a preliminary way, let us look at the creation. From the fact that God is *always Father*, but not always creator, we may see that it is *as Father* that he is creator. Barth tells us that '... the doctrine of creation answers that God, who does not need us, created heaven and earth and myself, of "sheer fatherly kindness and compassion, apart from any merit or worthiness of mine ..."' (Barth, p 54). **Understood like this, the doctrine of creation is a fundamental statement of belief.** 'Creation is grace: ... God does not grudge the existence of the reality distinct from himself' (Barth, p 54). Creation, then, is rooted in God's will not to exist for himself alone, but to share the fullness of his love with others. As Barth puts it: 'Creation is the temporal analogue, taking place outside God, of that event in God himself by which God is the Father of the Son. The world is not God's Son, is not "begotten" of God; but it is created. But what God does as the creator can in the Christian sense only be seen and understood as a reflection, as a shadowing forth of this inner divine relationship between God the Father and the Son' (Barth, p 52). Already, we are seeing the interplay between the doctrines of creation and the Trinity. This will be deepened as we proceed, but let us now turn to the incarnation.

The central importance of the incarnation is as the *real self-communication of God*, in Word and act. In Jesus Christ, God committed himself unreservedly to us in his own Triune being. The doctrines of the Trinity and the incarnation are interlinked, and as we trace out the

' ... the doctrine of creation is a fundamental statement of belief.'

trajectory of the incarnation, so our understanding of the Trinity is enriched.

Through the incarnation, God the Son made himself one of his own creatures. He entered and made his own the alienation of creation. Through his life, death and resurrection he brought *the love and power of God* to bear on its disorder, restoring it to God's love. As it is in Jesus that we are confronted by God, we understand that it is in Jesus that we *really* see the mystery of God's creative activity. In Jesus there is the new creation in the middle of the old, and this expands our understanding of the unique nature of God's creation, and the distinctive path of his love within it. As we are confronted with the nature and style of God's new creation in Jesus, we are able to understand the old creation as never before. In Jesus, the Saviour and Redeemer, we learn how the creator works, and through him, *the power* of God's love is shown as grace.

Let us look more closely at the life and works of Jesus. His birth, the incarnation, is a new act of God. God becomes man, without ceasing to be God. This is not a depotentiation of God, but a self-limitation, the exercise of his power *within* the limitations of our creaturely reality. Astonishingly, the power of God is shown in his willingness to become little.

And then there is the death of Christ. In this act, God enters and reaches into our extinction and non-being. Once again, we see here a further dimension to God's love and purpose, and so into the inner logic of his creative activity.

The resurrection of Jesus shows us the limitlessness, the constancy, the generosity and the hope of God's love. As nothing else, it shows the trajectory God's love takes. God's presence is healing, restoring, renewing, even out of rejection, alienation, emptiness and despair. With the resurrection, we see God's refusal to pass by, to ignore, to forget. There is nothing and nowhere out of which God is not redemptive.

Once again, the action of God in resurrection allows us to understand the action of the Triune God at a different and deeper level. If this is how God acts, it is how he will always act, and that in turn feeds into how we understand the action of God in creation. In the mission of Christ, *we see the utterly unexpected path the love and power of God takes.*

'As we are confronted with the nature and style of God's new creation in Jesus, we are able to understand the old creation as never before.'

God *loved* us so much that he gave up his only Son on our behalf; he accommodated himself to our smallness; by entering our extinction he undid the past to free us from our guilt.

In this process of identifying with, suffering, dying and rising again, we see the patience of the Creator with his creation. He chooses to display a power to restore and heal, not a power of coercion. At every step, we see God upholding, restoring and respecting the creaturely reality he has created. It is a process in which he safeguards the freedom he has given us, and undermines the power of evil by removing its victory and sting. The cross is the place of reconciliation, the hinge of his work – but we see that it is not the end. Christ rises again, and ascends to the right hand of the Father. This tells us that God's involvement in Christ with his creation was not a merely temporary phase, to be sloughed off like a snake's skin. Christ, clothed in his humanity, ever lives to intercede for us. He is the first-born of the new creation, who will bring many children to glory. So we see that the trajectory of his birth, life, death, resurrection and ascension reordered the creation. This was its purpose.

On the basis, now, of this fuller understanding of incarnation, let us turn back to the doctrine of **creation**. The fact that the world is not a necessary emanation from God, or necessarily co-eternal with him, but that which he created through his Son and the Spirit, means that he is able to come into relation to it, while remaining distinct from it. Another way of putting this is to say that God created the world, through his Son and the Spirit, in such a way that it is given a limited, but real independence of its own. It is not necessary, but contingent. It does exist, but it need not have existed.

Let us take this further, looking more closely at the nature of the creation's contingent reality. Because God creates through his Son and the Spirit, we may come to an understanding of the world that it is 'both real in itself and yet only itself in relation to its creator' (Gunton, *Christ* and Creation, 1992, p 75). Gunton here follows Thomas F Torrance. This is a theological understanding of the created world, which embraces human persons, the animal kingdom and the environment. It is given a real freedom and independence, but it does not contain its meaning in itself.

From looking at the incarnation, we have come to think of it as a dynamic initiative, the healing, restoring movement of God's love. Let us now apply this pattern of thinking to the doctrine of creation. God's involvement with that which he has made involves deliberate choice. It is an act of free grace, a deliberate act. But yet, like the incarnation, it is more than just an act. Quoting Colin Gunton again, 'it is also an enabling, because by that activity the world is given its own distinctive being and through the Spirit empowered to be the world, and not simply the tool or extension of deity' (Colin Gunton, p 78). It is here that we see again the significance of the world's contingent nature. It is given a real, but creaturely independence. This makes it real in itself, but it may only be itself in relation to its Creator. Gunton now takes this further. The fact that creation is in the Spirit as well as through the Son, allows us to see that creation has a purpose or goal. Gunton finds in this part of the meaning of the account of creation in six days: 'God creates freely, out of love, but it is a love which leaves the creature something to be and do: to live in time, to praise its creator and to return, perfected, to the one who made it' (Colin Gunton, p 77). The creation is not created and abandoned. Throughout, we have seen that this is never the path of God's love. Instead, the creation is creatively upheld and sustained in its existence beyond its own power in a relationship which both respects its freedom and brings it to its true purpose.

It follows that, as the Christian Church, we emphasise relationship rather than isolationism, personhood rather than individualism, and inter-relatedness springing from our understanding of the work of the Trinity in our creation and redemption. This is the theological basis for the practice of Christian medicine which must always seek to restore and heal, never to coerce or manipulate, and always to regard people as persons in communion with God and others.

> '... as the Christian Church, we emphasise relationship rather than isolationism, personhood rather than individualism, and inter-relatedness springing from our understanding of the work of the Trinity in our creation and redemption. This is the theological basis for the practice of Christian medicine which must always seek to restore and heal, never to coerce or manipulate.'

Summary

- **We have no knowledge of *who* God is, except through what he does.**

- Though God was always Father, he was not always Creator. The creation was a *new* act of God. To Christians, then, the creation is not 'just there'. We receive it with wonder as an instance of God's grace. 'The heavens declare the glory of God' (Psalm 19:1).

- God's act in Christ shows us the limitlessness, generosity and hope of God's love. Here we see the patience of the Creator with his creation. Entering into the depths of our emptiness and despair, he displays a power to restore and heal, never a power of coercion.

- In Christ we see humankind as God intended, in communion both with God and with other human persons.

- From this Trinitarian theology we draw a vision which affects how we relate to God, to other persons, and to the created world. *This is the basis of our ethics.* We, in our turn, are committed to live in costly communion with others, supporting the weak and the vulnerable. This is the basis of our critique of post-Enlightenment individualism. We are committed to receiving the world as *God's* world, allowing it to disclose itself (including its genetic structure) and forswearing manipulation, abuse and impatience.

It is this vision which gives us our commission, when faced with what is new.

Chapter 5
A PASTORAL PERSPECTIVE

On the issues of **consent** and **confidentiality** we have already tried, in contrast to the Nuffield Report, to approach from another perspective, to ask different, *specifically Christian* questions, which flow from our vision and his creation. Following this vision, we turn now to an expanded range of questions, believing that here too the Church may have a distinctive contribution to make. These are the questions of marriage, insurance, employment, our Christian acceptance of disability and our refusal to accept the tyranny of normality.

Screening and testing

The distinction between screening and testing

Screening may be applied to a whole population to find a condition or defect when there is no prior evidence of its presence in any individual, *eg* screening of new-born children for phenylketonuria. Testing, on the other hand, is applied to individuals when there is evidence that the condition may be present. Testing may also be carried out for individuals who have a relative suffering from a particular condition, or whose lifestyle puts them particularly at risk. However, the distinction is not always hard and fast, because the term 'screening' may also be applied in the case of a whole group of the population who are identified as being at particular risk for ethnic or other reasons. An example would be the screening of Ashkenazi Jews for the Tay-Sachs gene. This kind of selectivity of a particular group for screening will produce more accurate and more useful results than screening the whole population, and it also satisfies concerns about the unacceptably high cost of screening the whole population. However, for recessive diseases like cystic fibrosis, only a small proportion of gene carriers in the population will be identified by restricting testing to relatives of affected individuals.

The nature of the condition for which testing is being proposed may lead to difficult questions about the appropriate time for a test. Take the case of a disease whose onset is not until later life. Would it be proper to test a child, on the grounds that information obtained might help the child and its parents to make more informed decisions about educational opportunities and employment prospects; or would these possible advantages be outweighed by the resulting increase in anxiety that the tests would be bound to bring? When would it be appropriate to test offspring who could have inherited a defective gene from a parent? Would it be in childhood, in teenage years, or when, in the case of a woman, she is already pregnant, or, in the case of a man, his partner is already pregnant?

Screening and testing may raise different problems with regard to informed consent and the handling of unexpected and sometimes unwelcome information, and there will always be difficulties involved in testing children because a child cannot give proper consent.

The issue of consent

Before people can consent to any medical procedure they must be provided with information which is sufficient for them to give proper consent. Consent required for genetic tests is different to consent required for treatment. Those undergoing genetic testing have to be given sufficient information to enable them to think through the consequences of an abnormal result. While a patient in a surgery with his or her own general practitioner tends not to ask questions in depth about the purpose of any test suggested, the situation in a genetics department is very different. There, whether the patient seeks detailed information or not, the clinician will endeavour to ensure that the patient knows exactly what the test is for, and about the possible consequences. However, in both situations, individuals will vary as to the quantity and depth of information that they demand for their own peace of mind before they will give their consent. Their intellectual capacity will also be a determining factor as some people will be unable to assimilate more than the most basic information. A proportion will assume that the result will be normal and will not want to be worried by information they see as unnecessary. Others will be satisfied by the clinician inviting them to ask any questions, and assuring them that further information is available if required.

In the case of genetic screening or testing, people other than the patient may be involved; for example, other family members, a foetus, or other children not yet conceived. The availability of counselling is very important at all stages. Professionally-informed counselling ensures that definitive answers can be given to practical questions about the test itself, about the possible results and the possible options available thereafter, bearing in mind that there will often be no cure for the condition and the patient will often require help to come to terms with this. In the case of a test carried out on a pregnant woman which shows an affected foetus, the parents will require counselling to help them to decide whether or not to have a termination. They will have many questions to ask and some will come from reports they have read or seen on television of so-called 'miracle advances' which might result in successful treatment for their baby. The practitioner will require to strike a balance, on the one hand, between encouraging people to have hope and, on the other, being realistic, since the media are often over enthusiastic about reported advances. Some couples may consent to a test and, following a positive result, decide on a termination and immediately afterwards hear of a 'breakthrough'. They may feel cheated and wish that they had never consented to the test, since, without it, they would not have known that their child was affected and so would not have proceeded to termination.

All counselling, whether by professionals in the genetics field or by others, for example, ministers, must have the aim of helping individuals to reach a decision which is right for them and with which they are satisfied. This applies to making a decision whether or not to consent to testing, or to making a decision about how to cope with an abnormal result.

Counselling must always be seen to be as 'non-directive' as possible. In practice an entirely neutral stance may be impossible, if the issues are to be fully explored. However, it is very important that, at each stage, the individual is sure of what is happening and in particular knows that consent to screening or testing never implies consent to any subsequent treatment in the case of an abnormal result and, in particular, that there has been no consent to a termination of pregnancy.

Patients may often require counselling of a more general nature than that provided by the experts and they may seek this from their minister. Such counselling may be little more than a listening ear and great care is needed not to seem to be taking on the role of the professional, lest this cause confusion. However, individuals may need help if they feel pressured to take a course of action which they perceive to be in conflict with their Christian beliefs. Ministers will no doubt find themselves having to provide counselling in an ever increasing set of circumstances. Some questions may be an attempt to gain directional advice. For instance, should I bring a handicapped child into the world? Should I have a test in pregnancy? Should I have an abortion if that test result is abnormal? While the minister will always seek to avoid answering such questions directly, he or she may be more properly asked: where does the Church stand? How will any decision I make square with my Christian life and commitment?

Individuals seeking this kind of counselling from ministers will already have been given so much information by the medical and genetics experts that they are likely to feel both confused and, at least to a degree, in awe of the professionals. They are bound to know best. Perhaps it is here that as Christian counsellors we have something specific to offer. Our role must never be as the one who knows the answers, but as the one who can help them to an awareness of God's love for them, to an awareness that God is with them in whatever situation they are facing, however difficult, and eventually be the one who can help them reach a decision which is not only right for them, but which they feel they have made themselves.

Special care requires to be taken in the field of consent when dealing with minors, those who are mentally ill and those who have severe learning disabilities. The legal age of consent for medical treatment is 16, provided that the treatment is for the person's benefit. Below that age a child may consent if he or she has the ability to under-stand fully what is involved in the medical treatment or procedure (Gillick v DHSS (1986) A.C. 112). Otherwise permission must be given by a parent (not necessarily both parents) and it may only be given to promote the interests of the child. Therefore the genetic testing of children which is not of immediate benefit to them should be deferred until they can give proper consent. Similar considerations would apply in the case of the mentally ill or those with severe learning disabilities. It is difficult to see how proper consent could be obtained and so testing could probably only be seen as justified if the tests were of benefit to the individual. Levels of understanding will of course vary from individual to individual and each case will require to be considered on its own merits.

The issue of confidentiality

Genetic screening and testing takes the issue of confidentiality into a new realm. Confidentiality of information passed between patient and doctor has always been held as absolute – and rightly so, since without such a guarantee patients would have no trust in their doctors: if a patient was not assured of confidentiality he or she might well withhold important information which would be necessary for the doctor to make a proper diagnosis and prescribe appropriate treatment. Information given by the doctor to a patient can be passed on by the patient, but never by the doctor. In the past it was easier to safeguard confidentiality than at the present time. The large number of people required by modern technology to store and reproduce information makes matters more difficult and with the possibility of privatisation of areas such as secretarial services the situation will be even more difficult to control. However, it is a very sensitive area and, while recognising the practical difficulties, it is important that the concept of confidentiality should be treasured because it is important for patients' confidence. Genetic tests present new problems relating to confidentiality because such tests may reveal information not only about those who have consented to them, but also about other family members. Therefore, as well as having to consider how the confidentiality of such information is secured, those working in the field of genetics also have to consider the interests of other family members to whom the disclosure of information is as relevant as to the person tested. Their interests have to be balanced against the patient's right to absolute confidentiality, and if information is disclosed to them provision will require to be made for counselling as they may suddenly find themselves in possession of disturbing information.

The interests of family members in knowing the results of tests may clash with the wishes of the person who has been tested. Normally the rules of confidentiality should apply, but there will arise situations where the practitioner in counselling may seek to persuade someone to disclose information that they are reluctant to disclose because their failure to do so may be seriously disadvantageous to other family members. Persuasion must always be the means and not coercion.

One exception to the rule of confidentiality might be where disclosure is necessary to initiate urgent medical investigations for other family members. With careful counselling such occasions should be few and far between and they should be the rare exception to the rule of absolute confidentiality. It would be difficult, perhaps impossible, to legislate for such situations because each would have to be considered carefully on its merits so that the correct balance of interests may be struck. Common law will always allow disclosure of information if it is in the public interest. No doubt a body of interesting case law will develop as the question of whether something is or is not in the public interest is tested.

People other than health professionals will become involved in counselling and this will no doubt include ministers, to whom the same general principles of confidentiality apply. Difficult questions will be raised and it will be the task of the counsellor to help the person see that he or she has responsibilities to other people as well as rights. Sometimes the person may need reassurance. He or she may be afraid that disclosing information may make them somehow vulnerable, that only by guarding the secrets of their condition closely are they secure. Ministers here have a distinctive role, a role which seeks to help people understand that a condition from which they suffer is not a weakness and that disclosing it need not lead to shame and embarrassment. And a minister may be able to help a person in a practical way to pass on information to those who have a legitimate interest in it.

In considering the rights of family members to the disclosure of information, we must not forget that some people, far from seeking such information, would rather not receive it. Consider the situation when a young person checks for a condition because one of his or her grandparents has it. If the test is positive, the intervening generation may receive information they have not sought and have no desire to know.

A person may have particular reasons for not wanting to disclose information to family members at a particular time. Consider the situation of a woman who has had a test and discovered that she is a carrier of Duchenne Muscular Dystrophy. She may not want to pass that information on to a sister who is in the later stages of pregnancy.

She may find that keeping the information secret is very difficult and later may require help to tell her sister after the baby has been born. On the other hand, consider how the situation is changed if she were to have a sister who is soon to be married and likely to become pregnant. In that instance she might well want to pass the information on.

Issues of confidentiality are likely to become more and more difficult with the passage of time. Not only will more information be available, but the means by which it is stored will become more complicated and as such will require the involvement of progressively more and more people. We have come a long way from the doctor taking notes to which no-one else had access. Also the public's awareness about genetic screening and testing will grow, as will their awareness about the type and extent of information available. It may be that in future public pressure will result in a swing away from absolute confidentiality to give greater rights to interested parties.

Particular issues relating to marriage

Special problems might arise in marriage. Having suggested that only in very special circumstances could confidentiality be breached to pass on information to other members of a patient's family, it is necessary to ask if a prospective marriage partner should have any greater rights than other family members. An individual entering into marriage might want to withhold information about a genetic condition because he or she is afraid that there may be a chance that the other party will not wish to go ahead with the marriage. It might be argued that if the couple truly love each other the decision of one of them will not be affected by the disclosure of information relating to a genetic condition. But it must be at least possible that some people would be influenced in their decision if they were faced with the information that their partner and/or any children they might have could develop genetic disease.

A genetic condition is different from other illnesses. It is impossible for individuals to claim that their genes are theirs alone, since any blood relatives could carry the same defective gene. It follows that the discovery of a genetic abnormality will affect all the family, both present and not yet born.

Clearly if information becomes available only after the marriage has taken place, no fault can be attributed. The couple will require counselling as to how to deal with this unwelcome news, but it is to be hoped that they will be able to give help to each other. Their marriage vows will have bound them for better or worse, and while the emergence of such information will no doubt put a strain on a marriage, it could never be regarded by the Christian as a grounds for divorce.

Any question of genetic testing before marriage to check out the existence of abnormalities would have to be resisted, since that could change the whole fabric of relationships, with people perhaps becoming willing only to enter into marriage with people free from certain disease genes. As Christians our view of marriage is not only that it is for life, but also that it is founded on unconditional self-giving and sustained by grace. With rapid advances in the genetics field, the possibility of obtaining 'genetic profiles' may not be as far-fetched as the idea sounds. As Christians we would want to resist strongly anything which might result in genetic information becoming a consideration for entering into marriage.

The situation may be seen rather differently when one of the partners withholds such information which is in his possession prior to marriage. Such information is clearly relevant and to withhold it constitutes deception. A partner might feel very bitter when discovering this information after marriage. It is likely to strike at the base of the relationship, a relationship based on mutual love and trust. To find out that a marriage partner has knowingly withheld this information may lead the other partner to seek to terminate the marriage. How is a minister to respond when asked how the Church would regard divorce under such circumstances? On a legal basis it would probably not be difficult to establish that the relationship had broken down and that breakdown was irretrievable. It might be difficult to argue that the failure to give information of such an important nature is less significant behaviour than many other kinds of behaviour that have become accepted as constituting the basis for divorce. Divorce is legal recognition that a marriage relationship has

'As Christians our view of marriage is not only that it is for life, but also that it is founded on unconditional self-giving and sustained by grace.'

already foundered and so it would be a matter of establishing the fact of the breakdown. Some people might argue that the failure to disclose such information is so serious as to render the marriage voidable on the grounds that consent to marriage had been improperly obtained. A minister confronted with such a problem will seek to explore all possible courses of action with the couple.

Clearly many different questions could arise for counsellors and ministers counselling someone who has information; counselling couples who are struggling with information prior to marriage; and, most difficult of all, counselling those who find their marriage devastated by the emergence of information. As in the areas discussed earlier, the minister's task will be to help people to a decision which is right for them. There will never be easy answers.

Employment

In any employment situation the interests of an employer and an employee are likely to differ. An employer has a business to run, wants to run it efficiently, and particularly in a bad economic climate, will be anxious not to lose business to a competitor who is more efficient. In a time of high unemployment, and especially in a time where there are large numbers of people with skills who are unemployed, an employer can pick and choose among prospective employees. One of the ways to try to ensure maximum efficiency is to try to employ workers who do not have a record of being frequently absent from work on medical grounds. There are a wide range of pre-employment practices. At one end of the scale some employers ask for no more than a verbal statement; at the other end each applicant must complete a detailed statement of medical history for scrutiny by a medical practitioner designated by the employing authority, at the same time giving permission for information to be sought from his or her own GP. In the latter instance the designated medical officer will decide as to whether or not a medical examination is necessary. In some instances full medical examination is a necessary precondition to appointment irrespective of previous medical history. The determinants giving rise to such a variable code of practice are factors such as likelihood of recurrent periods of incapacity, length of contract, superannuation status, risk potential in the job situation, and so on. An employer has a legal responsibility to provide a safe working environment for employees, and it may be that an applicant is unsuitable for a particular job because of a condition from which he or she suffers. An employer also has to take into account other employees and he will not want to employ someone who may cause one of them an injury.

An employee making a job application is clearly looking for a job and is also looking for job security and for a job which is suitable for him or her. It might therefore be in his or her interests to undergo a medical examination which would show that the job for which he or she had applied was perhaps not suitable.

The above general principles will apply to genetic disease, but clearly people will be concerned that, with the increase in screening programmes, there will be more occasions when an employer can discriminate against a prospective employee. As in all cases where someone fails to gain employment, it would be difficult to determine whether or not this is discrimination. This has caused difficulties in cases of alleged discrimination on grounds of either sex or race, and much the same difficulties could arise for someone with a genetic disease. It is always open to an employer to show that the aggrieved person was not the successful applicant simply because there were other better qualified and more suitable applicants. The onus of proof would always be on the person alleging discrimination. However, an area of greater concern is for the prospective applicant who has been shown in a genetic test to be a carrier, and this information comes to the attention of the employer. The concern will be that employers will not understand that it is not relevant in considering whether or not to employ the particular person, since it would have no effect whatsoever on his or her ability to do the job in question. Employers may not have the knowledge to make this judgement, and they may not seek it either, preferring to act 'on the safe side'.

Although a person's genetic constitution cannot be altered by their working environment, the actual symptoms of a disease might be precipitated by their work situation. Also, someone who already

' ... people will be concerned that, with the increase in screening programmes, there will be more occasions when an employer can discriminate against a prospective employee.'

has the symptoms of a genetic disease will be likely to experience difficulties at work as the disease progresses. Its development may have implications for the way in which the individual can carry out the job, it may also have implications for safety in the workplace, and of course it may result in the individual being absent on frequent occasions.

As well as the interests of the individuals involved in offering or obtaining employment it is also important to take into account the public interest. While it might be considered generally a good thing to introduce genetic screening if it could be shown to decrease the incidence of occupational disease, concern would be raised if what eventually happened was that certain individuals were excluded from employment because of genetic screening. It is not a new idea to exclude certain individuals from employment on health grounds. The concern is that genetic screening might identify a whole new class of person – those at high risk of developing a late onset condition, or carriers of a disease gene who will themselves remain healthy – and that they might be discriminated against, and such discrimination could be based on fear, prejudice and misunderstanding.

As in other areas, these problems are not real at this time. But increased use of genetic screening, coupled with harder drives for maximum efficiency from employees, may eventually make it a very real problem.

Insurance

Here, as in the issue of employment, we are faced with differing interests, *ie* the insurance companies and those seeking life insurance. Each one of us, when applying for life insurance, hopes to have the application considered favourably and hopes that he or she will obtain the insurance cover sought at the lowest price. If we suffer from any medical condition that the insurance company considers relevant, then we are required to pay more than someone who does not suffer from any such condition. Our desire to obtain the cheapest possible insurance is at least partly responsible for the weighting on some policies. No doubt if we were all prepared to pay more for our life

'The concern is that genetic screening might identify a whole new class of person – those at high risk of developing a late onset condition, or carriers of a disease gene who will themselves remain healthy – and that they might be discriminated against.'

'… increased use of genetic screening, coupled with harder drives for maximum efficiency from employees, may eventually make it a very real problem.'

insurance, then there would be no need for such weighting and we would all pay the same. Insurance companies are seeking to provide insurance cover, but they are also trying to generate revenue. For them it is important to know at least the identifiable risks for each person seeking insurance. Those who are suffering from ill health, or those who are likely to suffer from certain conditions because of their family histories, are the people who are likely to cost the insurance companies the most money. The insurance companies charge them an increased premium to take account of the identified increased risk. Their principal concern is how a condition will affect life expectancy, and the same is true of any condition that they may develop in the future.

Further there are the interests of professionals working in the field of genetic screening and testing. There are fears that there might be pressure to reveal the results of tests to insurance companies, but as far as we know this has never happened. They are also concerned that people may be afraid to have tests, because if the result were adverse this would be likely to have an effect on their insurance prospects, and their business might depend on obtaining insurance. Again, this is something that has not yet materialised.

Many ethical issues will emerge in the field of insurance from genetic screening and testing. It is well established and accepted that proposal forms ask not only about recent medical treatment, but also relevant elements of family history. It is also well established that insurance companies have the right to ask for the applicant's permission to approach his or her general practitioner with a view to securing an extract of their medical records, and the results of any genetic tests would be incorporated therein. However, it might be considered less acceptable that they should have access to information that might show that an applicant will develop a late onset condition: for example, Huntington's disease. Similarly, a person whose father died of Huntington's disease might be pressurised into having tests and that may also be considered less acceptable. There seems at the present time no evidence of insurance companies pressurising people into having such tests. An applicant facing such a requirement would be justified in 'shopping around' to find a better deal: given the highly

'There are fears that there might be pressure to reveal the results of tests to insurance companies, but as far as we know this has never happened.'

'Many ethical issues will emerge in the field of insurance from genetic screening and testing.'

'... it might be considered less acceptable that they should have access to information that might show that an applicant will develop a late onset condition: for example, Huntington's disease.'

competitive conditions that exist between insurance companies, he or she would be likely to obtain one. It would seem unfair that an applicant suffering from a condition for which a test has been developed should be discriminated against over an applicant who is genetically predisposed to a condition for which no test has yet been developed.

But there is another side to this – namely that a situation could arise whereby an applicant could have a test and then be able to say categorically that he was not suffering from, nor would he ever suffer from, such a condition as Huntington's disease. This might put such an applicant in an advantageous position when compared to the other applicants who could not show in some way that they would not one day suffer from heart disease, for example.

At the present time the information sought in a proposal form is fairly wide reaching about the applicant's health. Someone applying for insurance is requested to complete a questionnaire relating to episodes of illness or incapacity and family history; coupled with this a signature is required for consent for the family doctor to be approached. In most instances the family doctor receives a form for completion which involves an extract from records. This does not involve that doctor in making any statement as to the patient's eligibility for acceptance or otherwise for the purposes of insurance. This report is subsequently sent to the Medical Referee for that insurance company. On the basis of the applicant's statement and the family doctor's report, a decision is made as to whether or not an examination is required or further information is necessary. If examination is required, it is normally carried out by a practitioner other than the applicant's own doctor, who will be asked to pass an opinion and pass his or her findings to the Medical Referee with whom the final decision rests.

The advances in genetics are bound to raise fears in people that here is another area of information to which the insurance company has a legitimate right to access. Many conditions cannot be screened for before their onset. There are no more conditions around now than previously, it is simply that sometimes individuals who will develop them can now be identified before disease onset. However, it seems at the present time that insurance companies have no intention of including an additional question asking specifically for the results of

'The advances in genetics are bound to raise fears in people that here is another area of information to which the insurance company has a legitimate right to access.'

genetic testing. Compare this with the inclusion in recent years of a specific question relating to HIV and AIDS. However, there is a section in the application which asks the applicant if there is anything further in his or her medical history or family history which is relevant to his or her present application. A person who had received an adverse test result would have an obligation to disclose it at this point in the form. Given this policy on test results, it seems most unlikely that insurance companies will require tests as a prerequisite to a person obtaining insurance. It is unlikely that public opinion would allow them to do so.

Genetic testing and the Law

There will always be those who think that the law ought to be able to govern every area of our lives, and that the law ought to be clear in all instances. This black and white approach is well nigh impossible to achieve in practice. In every situation, grey areas will emerge. It is very doubtful whether it would be desirable for legislation to attempt to cover every possibility, as it would be difficult for the law to develop when information advanced. This seems particularly true in the field of genetics, where advances seem to be happening particularly fast.

At first glance it might seem that the easiest area for which to legislate would be the legal protection of genetic information. Common Law and Statute (Data Protection Act, 1984) protect the confidentiality of medical information. But we have seen earlier that the issue of confidentiality is by no means simple and the general principle may have to be laid aside in certain cases in the public interest. It would be impossible for legislation to itemise all the possible circumstances, as each case will have to be considered on its merits.

When we come to areas such as insurance and employment, the issues are again complex. Legislation could never foretell all the circumstances that might arise. The law will develop as cases come before the courts and are decided, sometimes being tested in the highest courts in the land. This is almost law-making by the courts and it puts enormous pressures on the judges. It also means that the litigants before the courts can be subject to the idiosyncrasies of the judges. It may be that legislation can come after a series of decisions. These may be good decisions and legislation may seek to formalise them. They may be bad decisions which have brought widespread condemnation and legislation may seek to rectify them.

It can be clearly envisaged that many interesting cases will come before the courts – not too far in the future – perhaps in employment or insurance, where people feel they have been unfairly treated and seek to show discrimination, or in the field of family law: *eg* divorces based on the decision not to disclose genetic information before marriage. Such cases may have far-reaching effects – on the existing children of a marriage, and the financial situations of both parties.

Involvement in litigation can bring its own stresses, distinct from those arising from the situation giving rise to the litigation. People are afraid of getting too involved in the law, but may feel that this is the only possible way to get what they see as their right. Such stresses and uncertainties will no doubt give rise to pastoral problems, and they may be combined with, say, the stress of not finding a job and the stress of also finding out about the existence of a genetic condition.

Stigmatisation and Disability

Traditionally the Church, through the work of the Board of Social Responsibility, has offered imaginative care to the disadvantaged and disabled. At a national level the Board offers residential care and on-going respite care to families in a number of centres including Keith Lodge, Stonehaven, and the new purpose-built unit called The Mallard at Springburn, Glasgow. Such units care for young people with profound mental and physical problems. In Lanarkshire, the Cornerstone Project provides care in small groups for adults who would otherwise be hospitalised for the duration of their lives.

Underlying this care is the Christian view that all people are made in God's image, and are precious in his sight. The image of God is not distorted in the weak, the disabled or those suffering from genetic illness. Jürgen Moltmann has the view that there is really no such thing as 'the handicapped'. There are only people – people who have this or that difficulty, which makes the society of the strong and capable unjustly label them as 'handicapped'.

In the dilemmas of genetic screening and testing, Christians must offer people choices that are right for them. As genetic screening increases, there must be a concern that pressure will be brought to bear on parents not to have the children who are diagnosed before birth as suffering from disability. Maureen Ramsey points to this danger: 'So if a woman decides against prenatal screening or abortion when she is found to be carrying a foetus with a genetic defect, it becomes her shame, her guilt, her responsibility for the way the baby turns out. The end result becomes not her fate, but her fault' (*Genetic Counselling: Practice and Principles*, 1994, p 253).

Parents may decide not to terminate a pregnancy, and such a decision may be contrary to the advice of professionals who may feel pressurised by the financial restraints of the NHS. They may feel isolated at having a child who is regarded by others as 'a burden on society'. Such stigmatisation is anathema to Christians. Pastorally, parents making such a decision should receive support and confirmation, and continuing support as the child grows. We should not underestimate the anguish parents face in such circumstances. As one mother of a severely handicapped son (Professor Frances Young of Birmingham University) wrote for the Study Group: 'If I'd known in advance what our lives would hold I couldn't have faced it – his distress and my answering distress have at times been unbearable. But I thank God I was never faced with a decision about abortion ....'

Society in general is adopting a hypocritical approach to the disabled. While buildings and public places are rightly being altered and adapted for the use of the disabled, financial resources socially and medically are in danger of being diverted from their care. Lack of knowledge about certain conditions, particularly the less well publicised ones, can lead to a lack of understanding as to what restrictions in living the individual has.

Does the Church take seriously whether the disabled person can join other people around the communion table? Or are the physical restrictions too great? What of the embarrassment a carer may feel

'Christians must offer people choices that are right for them. As genetic screening increases, there must be a concern that pressure will be brought to bear on parents not to have the children who are diagnosed before birth as suffering from disability.'

'... stigmatisation is anathema to Christians.'

Frances Young comments: 'I thank God I was never faced with a decision about abortion.'

when a disabled person disturbs other worshippers? Whilst physical barriers can be removed, attitudes are more difficult to change.

For the Church the disabled must be more than objects of care. Frances Young speaks of disabled people belonging to society, not just through acceptance, but in being able to contribute. If they are truly to be persons, we must learn to receive from them.

Society can offer not only care to those who are disabled, but also the opportunity to influence decision-making on the care. Grampian Regional Council has implemented Sections 1 and 2 of the Disabled Persons Act. These give the disabled user of services the right to have an advocate or representative to speak on their behalf and help them in their dealings with staff, thus influencing decisions. Christians may feel this is a way of empowering and giving choice to disabled people.

The Church must be sensitive to the fears of families about future care of loved ones and affirm the importance of adequate provision for them. The growing emphasis on care in the community, while it has a positive, imaginative and exciting side, also requires careful monitoring to ensure that proper funding and facilities are not only made available, but continue to be available.

Chapter 6
CONCLUSION

The Board of Social Responsibility's aim in preparing this book has been to put human genetics in perspective. Contemporary developments and issues in human genetics have been set within an informed and balanced scientific perspective and a distinctive theological and pastoral perspective, all within the wider perspective of the public debate on bioethics. In a fast-changing discipline like human genetics, it is not possible to offer final conclusions. However, it is desirable to have such a responsible Christian perspective to offer the Church, and to offer our wider society guidance on an important topic that will increasingly affect all our lives. In this book, the Board of Social Responsibility has drawn attention to how future work should be undertaken to stimulate further thought and action by the Church. It is appropriate, then, that the last word should go to a Church member and close relative of a child with cystic fibrosis, who offered the Board of Social Responsibility Study Group on Human Genetics this personal testimony:

You ask for comment on the 'predicament' of families facing cystic fibrosis, but there are two. There's the day-to-day predicament and, for want of a better word, the theological one.

The day-to-day one is more easily defined and so unfairly allotted. It seems so cruel a burden on young parents. Grandparents and others might have shared it more when extended families were situated to give more mutual support. But we're hundreds of miles away, not up a close round the corner.

We learn to welcome good intentions and kind words that go wrong because inevitably the well-wishers repeat each other. They so obviously wish they could remember just what was that more hopeful story about research they read in the papers; and they all say: 'There's so much more can be done nowadays.' Yes, but .... Besides, we feel guilty ourselves.

For me it's not just guilt – mixed with relief perhaps – that we can't be there to help with the physio and the daily worries. At long range it's easy to put the best gloss on things, always believing reassuring words on the phone about infections and minor illnesses, awkward enough with 'normal' children. We worry, and weep inwardly, but at our age our working and leisure lives or career prospects won't be overshadowed and possibly affected by the strains. But for the parents?

Maybe we subconsciously avoid long-term worries too. Like parents, we live in hope that medical progress already extending life expectation for CF sufferers will continue at its recent rate, even achieve the Great Breakthrough. But perhaps we secretly hope to opt out; to be gone before the troubles of CF childhood, mitigated by love and protective care, give way to the limitations and limited expectations of the teenage and young adult years.

I feel guilty about the extent to which grandparents can shut it out or switch it off. Even in insisting that we're treating all the family alike, we may help the pretence that they are all alike.

Yet I ought to believe that ultimately we are all alike, dependent on grace and with whatever equality of opportunity for eternity is consistent with what Paul says about predestination. I wish I did more firmly, and that may be a factor in feeling guilty about the theological predicament. Is it because my faith isn't strong enough that it's not tested more?

Ought I to be railing against the Almighty, asking how unfairness fits into his perfect love, wondering how our girl will react to the Gospel miracles of healing? At the very least, should I not be setting out to do a Milton and justify the ways of God to man? Instead there are different reactions amid the silent tears. A new insight into the power of love; a new sense of the uniqueness of human personality; a new scepticism about arguments for terminating a life once conceived. Perhaps also, amid unavoidable perplexity, a new revelation of the aptness of seeing God as our Father. Whatever else my grand-daughter is denied, I think (as I watch her parents cope) she will surely grasp the power of that metaphor, and also of the love of Mary for the child with so strange a destiny.

' ... amid unavoidable perplexity, a new revelation of the aptness of seeing God as our Father.'

Allele
Any one of the alternative forms of a specified gene. Different alleles of the same gene may have different phenotypic expression.

Amino Acid
A chemical structure which forms the basic building block of proteins. Twenty different amino acids occur naturally and each protein has different characteristics depending on how the amino acids are strung together. The strings are called polypeptide chains, and tend to bunch and coil up to produce complex shapes essential for biological function. The order in which amino acids are built is decided by genes.

Autosome
Any one of the 22 matched pairs of chromosomes, one of each is inherited from both mother and father; in contrast to the sex chromosomes.

Base
The name for nucleotides, the building blocks of DNA. The four bases are cytosine, adenine, thymine and guanine. When arranged in order along a chain they form a unique biological language with a four letter alphabet (C A T and G). Each group of three bases on a gene corresponds to one type of amino acid.

Carrier
A healthy individual who has both an abnormal and a normal copy of a pair of genes for a genetic disorder or characteristic.

Cell
The smallest living component of all organisms, usually with the capacity to grow and divide. Almost all cells contain genes contained in the cell nucleus.

Chromosomes
Strings of genes contained in the nucleus of the cell. Humans have 22 pairs of chromosomes, together with two sex chromosomes.

Clone　　　　　A group of genetically identical cells or organisms derived from a common ancestor.

Cytomegalovirus A fairly common virus which can be transmitted to a foetus by an infected mother. Infection of the foetus can cause severe developmental abnormalities.

DNA　　　　　Deoxyribose Nucleic Acid is the substance produced when strings of bases are built together to encode genetic information.

Dominant　　A trait or characteristic of a gene which is more active than another with which it is paired.

Enzyme　　　A protein that acts like a biological machine joining structures together, assembling structures, or tearing them apart.

Gamete　　　Sperm or egg cells containing half a complete set of genes, and used in the process of reproduction.

Gene　　　　A string of bases which contain instructions for building a particular polypeptide, usually to form a protein.

Gene therapy　An attempt to reprogram cells in the body to cure disease, or reduce symptoms.

Genetic disease　Medical problem resulting from an abnormal gene.

Genetic engineering　Human intervention designed to produce artificial changes in genetic code of organisms that could not be produced as quickly (if at all) by the normal techniques of interbreeding.

Genetic fingerprinting　A technique which enables genetic relationships between close relatives, or the identity of individuals to be established, usually beyond reasonable doubt.

Genetic marker　A harmless variable change in DNA or protein that can be used to locate a disease gene on a particular chromosome.

Genome

The totality of the DNA sequence of an organism.

Germ line

Germ line cells are cells which are specialised in the body to produce sperm or eggs. Reprogramming germ line cells has drastic consequences because offspring will inherit the changes, as will subsequent generations.

Human Genome Mapping Project

A major UK research initiative started in 1989 and coordinated by the Medical Research Council. It consists of a directed programme of research to map the human genome and a Resource Centre which is funded to maintain a collection of genetic resources for use by UK and other scientists. The UK's Genome Mapping Project is linked to similar projects in the USA, Europe and Japan, which coordinate their activities to avoid duplication.

Insertional mutagenesis

The process of changing a DNA sequence by inserting a new sequence or by replacing part of the original sequence with another sequence.

Multifactorial

A term which denotes that many factors, often environmental *eg* diet, contribute to the development of a disease.

Mutation

A change in the genetic code.

Nucleus

A bag of protein inside the cell containing genes arranged in chromosomes.

Phenotypic expression

The observable characteristic of an organism determined by a specific gene or allele, *eg* hair colour is the 'phenotypic expression' of the alleles coding for hair pigments carried by an individual.

PKU

Phenylketonuria; a single gene, inherited disorder. All new-born infants in the UK are screened at birth for this disorder using a blood test. Most of the serious side effects of this disorder can be avoided if affected individuals are kept on a special diet from infancy.

Protein

The sequences of genes are read as a code by the synthetic machinery of cells. The code corresponding to each gene is translated into a specific protein. All proteins consist of strings of amino acids, which are differentiated from one another by the sequence of the string, and by their functional properties. Some proteins act as metabolic catalysts, inside and outside cells. Others act as 'messenger molecules', carrying information from one part of the body to another. Still others have a structural role, such as the proteins which make up ligaments and muscles.

Probe

A short, single-stranded sequence of DNA or RNA which can be used to detect and evaluate the presence of related sequences, with some specificity for harmful versus normal alleles.

Recessive

A trait or characteristic of a gene which is never expressed or activated in the cell unless both genes in the pair of chromosomes coding for the activity are saying the same thing. A recessive trait may not be active therefore unless inherited from both parents.

Recombinant DNA

DNA made by joining (recombining) fragments of DNA together by genetic engineering techniques.

Ribosome

A protein building factory inside the cell, using RNA to determine the sequence of amino acids.

RNA

Ribonucleic acid is a similar structure to DNA and is made by copying DNA in the nucleus. RNA then moves out of the nucleus and is used to provide instructions for building proteins.

Somatic cell

A cell used by the body in life, but not giving rise to sperm or eggs.

Virus

An infectious agent-complex protein bag containing a small amount of genetic material (DNA or RNA) and enzymes to use the code to reprogram chromosomes inside the nucleus of cells. Many viruses cause disease, but others can be used as part of genetic experiments.

Zygote   Cell formed by the union of two gametes, *eg* a sperm and an egg uniting to form a fertilised egg poised to start dividing to form a whole human being.

X-linked   The form of inheritance in which the gene is carried on the X chromosome.

Appendix 2:
COMPOSITION of STUDY GROUP

The Study Group comprised:

* *Rev. Dr W F Storrar* (Convener), Lecturer in Practical Theology, University of Aberdeen.

Rev. Dr Iain Torrance (Secretary), Lecturer in Systematic and Practical Theology, University of Aberdeen.

Dr Susan Holloway, Research Worker in Clinical Genetics.

Dr Jane Bower, Senior Lecturer in Management Studies (with experience of research in molecular genetics), University of Aberdeen.

Dr Donald M Bruce, Director of the Church of Scotland Society, Religion and Technology Project.

Mrs Ann Allen, Teacher, Vice-Convener of the Board of Social Responsibility.

* *Mrs Helen M McLeod*, an Elder, experienced in academic research.

* *Rev. David J C Easton*, Minister of Burnside Parish, Glasgow.

* *Rev. John D Whiteford*, Minister of Stonehaven Dunnottar Parish.

* *Rev. Ann Inglis*, Associate Minister of Corstorphine Craigsbank, Edinburgh, and an Advocate.

Dr W S Hossack, Medical Practitioner.

[* Members of the Board of Social Responsibility.]

The Study Group on Human Genetics benefited from links with the Society, Religion and Technology Working Group on Non-Human Genetic Engineering, and with the Board of Social Responsibility Study Group on Human Fertilisation and Embryology.

Appendix 3:
ACKNOWLEDGMENTS

Association of British Insurers, 51 Gresham Street, London, EC2V 7HQ.

Rev. Dr N G Messer.

Dr David Porteous, Head of Molecular Genetics, MRC Human Genetics Unit, Edinburgh.

Dr Mary Porteous, Clinical Genetics Unit, Western General Hospital, Edinburgh.

Emeritus Professor Margaret Stacey, formerly Professor of Sociology, University of Warwick.

Professor Frances Young, University of Birmingham.

The Board of Social Responsibility thanks all members of its Study Group on Human Genetics for their full contribution in producing this report. In publishing the report for a wider readership, the Board acknowledges the particular contribution of the following members who wrote specific sections:

Dr Jane Bower (chapter 2).

Dr Iain Torrance (chapters 3, 4).

Rev. Ann Inglis (chapter 5).

Dr Susan Holloway (glossary).